Love Letters: Dutch Genre Paintings in the Age of Vermeer

Love Letters: Dutch Genre Paintings in the Age of Vermeer

Bruce Museum of Arts and Science
Greenwich, Connecticut
National Gallery of Ireland
Dublin

Letters

Dutch Genre Paintings in the Age of Vermeer

Peter C. Sutton
Lisa Vergara
Ann Jensen Adams
with Jennifer Kilian and Marjorie E. Wieseman

This catalogue is published in conjunction with the
exhibition *Love Letters: Dutch Genre Paintings in the Age
of Vermeer* organized by the Bruce Museum of Arts and
Science, Greenwich, Connecticut, and the National
Gallery of Ireland, Dublin
October 1 – December 31, 2003, Dublin
January 31 – May 2, 2004, Greenwich

ISBN 0-9720736-6-3

Printed in Singapore by CS Graphics

Catalogue design: Anne von Stuelpnagel
Editor: Fronia W. Simpson
Proofreader: Nancy Ross
Exhibition Coordination: Kathy Reichenbach (BM)
                         Fionnuala Croke (NGI)
                         Susan O'Connor (NGI)
Registrars: Meghan Tierney (BM)
            Elizabeth Duignan (NGI)

Cover:
Cat. 5. Gerard ter Borch
Woman Writing a Letter (detail), c. 1655
Monogrammed on the table: *GTB*
Oil on panel, 39 x 29.5 cm
Royal Cabinet of Paintings, Mauritshuis,
The Hague, no. 797

Contents

Welcome

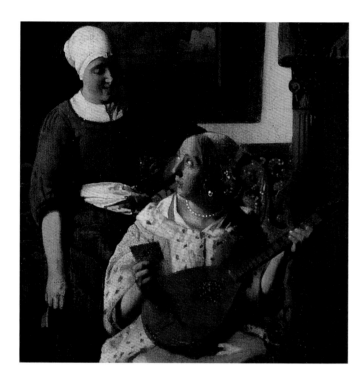

As a global company with a special appreciation for the things in life that are truly priceless, MasterCard International is pleased to support an initiative that brings world-renowned art to local communities.

Love Letters: Dutch Genre Painting in the Age of Vermeer is a unique exhibition focusing on the theme of letter writing in seventeenth-century Dutch art.

Organized by the Bruce Museum in Greenwich, Connecticut, in cooperation with the National Gallery of Ireland in Dublin, this landmark international exhibition includes the works of Dutch masters Johannes Vermeer, Pieter de Hooch, and Gerard ter Borch, among others. Many of the paintings in the exhibit are gathered from private art collections in Europe and the United States.

The images in *Love Letters: Dutch Genre Painting in the Age of Vermeer* vividly capture the importance of literacy and letter writing in Holland during the seventeenth century, a time when few would predict that technology would eventually make thoughtfully crafted, handwritten correspondence the exception rather than the rule.

At MasterCard, we strive to uncover the things in life that truly matter to consumers around the world. Our research indicates that core values and traditions – similar to those conveyed in these paintings – have remained of fundamental importance to people from generation to generation. We are confident that artists, scholars, and the general public alike will appreciate and enjoy this exhibit's extraordinary images, which warmly chronicle the traditional art of letter writing through the eyes of the great Dutch masters.

Robert W. Selander
President and Chief Executive Officer
MasterCard International

Cat. 38 bis, detail

$\mathcal{S}$ponsors

At the Bruce Museum, the exhibition and its catalogue are generously underwritten by

VNU

Mr. and Mrs. Norman Hascoe
Mr. and Mrs. George Landegger
Jean and David W. Wallace

Samuel H. Kress Foundation
Malcolm Hewitt Wiener Foundation
David T. Langrock Foundation
Netherland–America Foundation

Marsh Private Client Services

COMMITTEE OF HONOR

Honorary Chairman
His Excellency, Ambassador Boudewijn van Eenennaam

VERMEER CIRCLE
Anonymous
Mr. and Mrs. Rob van den Bergh
Mr. and Mrs. Thomas P. Clephane
Mr. and Mrs. George Crapple
Mr. and Mrs. Ray Dalio
Mr. and Mrs. David Darst
French & Company
Mr. and Mrs. Don Gaston
Mr. and Mrs. Lane Grijns
Mr. Bob Haboldt
Albert Kenworthy, Mary Mattson and sons
Ms. Susan E. Lynch
Mr. and Mrs. Frans van der Minne
Mr. and Mrs. Stephen Munger
Mr. Otto Naumann
Mr. Rob Noortman
Mr. and Mrs. Bernard Palitz

Mrs. Munroe F. Pofcher
Dr. and Mrs. James Reibel
Mr. and Mrs. Dirk Sturrop
Mr. and Mrs. Paul R. C. Sullivan
Mr. Johnny Van Haeften
Mr. Adam Williams

BENEFACTORS
A.D. Lines-Eurogroup, Inc.
Mr. Konrad O. Bernheimber, Bernheimber-Colnaghi
Mrs. Judith Lund Biggs
Mr. and Mrs. Cees Bruynes
Mr. and Mrs. Nathaniel B. Day
Mr. and Mrs. Michael Enthoven
Mr.and Mrs. Martin S. Feldstein
Carl and Sabrina Forsythe
Mr. Jack Kilgore, Kilgore and Company
Mr. and Mrs. Thomas Melly
Mr. and Mrs. Mario Ponce
Mr. and Mrs. Henry Scherer
Mr. and Mrs. Jean Pierre Van Rooy

PATRONS
Orde Van Der Prince Afdeling Manhattan
Blake Elin Vanderlip Memorial Foundation
Mrs. Henry A. Ashforth, Jr.
Mr. William S. Bucknall
Mr. and Mrs. George Case
Mr. and Mrs. Bruce F. Cohen
Mr. and Mrs. Joel C. Coleman
Mr. and Mrs. Maurits E. Edersheim
Mr. and Mrs. Richard Huber
Mr. and Mrs. Steven Levy
Mr. and Mrs. Peter Mitchell
Mr. and Mrs. James X. Mullen
Mrs. James E. Osborn II
The Pelgrift Family
Professor Martin Peretz
Mr. and Mrs. Homer Rees
Mrs. Jacques A. S. Robbins
Mr. and Mrs. Robert J. Rukeyser
Mrs. Marei von Saher
Mrs. Deborah Stiles
Mrs. Anna Glen Vietor
Mr. and Mrs. John W. Watling
Mr. and Mrs. Robert H. Whitby
Mr. Tom Wysmuller

List in formation

Preface

In an age of unsolicited junk mail, electronic "spam," and pop-ups, the receipt of an actual handwritten letter has become an occasion. If one omits business correspondence – invoices, contracts, legal communications, solicitations, payment notices, and the like – formal invitations to social events (an engraved invitation to a party, wedding or funeral), and the occasional thank-you note, personal letters have become rare, even quaint. Especially in recent years, they have been replaced by the burgeoning urgency of e-mail, with its own laconic and rapidly evolving style, syntax and jargon. The immediacy and alacrity of e-mail has the virtue of keeping all of us in instant touch, as well as the advantage (or disadvantage, as court cases have revealed) over once-dominant voice-mail of leaving a permanent written record of personal communication. In this accelerated climate, we enjoy something of the pithy brevity of telegraphic correspondence, when Dorothy Parker could write: "Arrived in Venice. Streets full of water. Please advise." But by the same token, the breathless instantaneity of twenty-first century written communication discourages reflection and formality; one taps a hasty, often half-considered reply, and presses "Send." Indeed so pervasive is the personal computer's dominance of business and private correspondence that the personal secretary has become virtually endangered.

And yet the postman still calls and delivers, bringing us the occasional handwritten private letter, the impact of which is all the more vivid and powerful for its novelty, manual craft and evidence of the personal touch. A letter can evoke unhurried, bygone times when long days and nights featuring fewer distractions and entertainments afforded (and social conduct required) greater literary consideration and effort. People composed letters with care and savored their messages, often repeatedly. The present exhibition examines a group of the very first images that recorded this fascination with letters. In the seventeenth century the Dutch made the letter a recurrent, even central, feature of their art, developing it as an aspect of their pictorial record of daily life in the home, which they celebrated in art before and to a greater extent than all other nationalities and peoples. The pictures in this show thus form a homogeneous whole that explores the various permutations and associations of the letter theme. Subsequent schools of painting took Dutch genre paintings as their point of departure. Thus we are indebted to the Dutch for having first lent form to this charming and enduring subject.

However the organizers of this exhibition owe their greatest debt to the lenders, without whose consent the show could never have been realized. Their public-spiritedness in temporarily sacrificing the pleasure of their art to share these works with our museum visitors is admirable. At the Bruce Museum, we also are very grateful to MasterCard International who have generously agreed to serve as lead corporate sponsor for the showing of the exhibition at the Bruce Museum. The welcome letter by Robert W. Selander, CEO of MasterCard International, appears here. In addition we wish to thank the following corporate sponsors: VNU, Heineken, and Marsh Private Client Services for their exceptional support of the exhibition. Suzanne and Norman Hascoe, George and Eva Landegger, Jean and David Wallace, the Samuel H. Kress Foundation, the Malcolm Hewitt Wiener Foundation, the David T. Langrock Foundation, and the Netherland–America Foundation also generously supported the planning and implementation of the exhibition and the catalogue. Heartfelt thanks are also extended to the many individuals who agreed to support the show through their membership on the Committee of Honor in the United States, headed by the Dutch Ambassador to the U.S., Boudewijn van Eenennaam. The names of these wonderfully generous and enthusiastic supporters are listed on a previous page. Their personal beneficence and large numbers have been an especially gratifying source of encouragement to everyone who has worked on the show. In Dublin we wish to thank His Excellency, the Dutch Ambassador to Ireland, J. van der Velden and his colleagues for their assistance; Minister John O'Donoghue TD, and the Department for Arts, Sports and Tourism for their ongoing support of the Gallery's exhibition programme.

Raymond Keaveney
Director
National Gallery of Ireland
Dublin

Peter C. Sutton
Executive Director
Bruce Museum
Greenwich

Cat 19, detail

Acknowledgments

Any project of this scale incurs many debts. I wish to first thank my very able co-authors, Lisa Vergara and Ann Jensen Adams, for their welcome essays, and Marjorie E. Wieseman and Jennifer Kilian for assisting with such celerity on the entries. My good colleagues in Dublin, Fionnuala Croke and Susan O'Connor, kept track of the many loan requests and deftly administrated the negotiations with lenders. The catalogue was expertly edited by Fronia W. Simpson, and designed with her customary flair and attention to detail by Anne von Stuelpnagel. Kathy Reichenbach was indispensable in organizing the manuscript and gathering photographs. Meghan Tierney and Elizabeth Duignan oversaw the logistical challenges of the show. York Baker and her team worked tirelessly to secure support for the exhibition. In addition, many others provided valuable advice or assistance. Among those we wish to acknowledge are Brenda and Thomas Brod, Anthony Crichton-Stuart, Frits Duparc, Jan Piet Filedt Kok, Michael Fitzgerald, Eddy van Geelen, Johnny van Haeften, Ben Hall, J. J. Havelaar, Annewies van den Hoek, G. Hoogsteeger, Jack Kilgore, Susan Donahue Kuretsky, Friso Lammertse, Ronald de Leeuw, Walter Liedtke, J. M. Montias, Otto Naumann, Rob Noortman, Paul Raison, Maria A. Schenkeveld-van der Dussen, Paul Tucker, George Wachter, Arthur K. Wheelock Jr., Clovis Whitfield, Adam Williams, and Jim Wright. Finally, for sustaining the august research facilities that enable us to compile a catalogue such as this, the Rijksbureau voor Kunsthistorische Documentatie and Koninklijke Bibliotheek in The Hague, the Witt Library in London, and the Frick Art Reference Library and the New York Public Library are gratefully acknowledged.

Peter C. Sutton 2003

Lenders

Accademia Carrara di Belle Arti, Bergamo
Thos. Agnew's and Sons Ltd., London
Alte Pinakothek, Bayerische Staatsgemäldesammlungen,
    Munich
Sarah Campbell Blaffer Foundation, Houston
Museum Boijmans Van Beuningen, Rotterdam
Marquis of Bute
Musée Fabre, Montpellier
Fondation Aetas Aurea
Gemäldegalerie Alte Meister, Staatliche
    Kunstsammlungen, Dresden
Gemäldegalerie Alte Meister, Staatliche Museen, Kassel
The Menil Collection, Houston
The Metropolitan Museum of Art, New York
William Morrison Collection, Sudeley Castle,
    Gloucestershire
National Gallery of Art, Washington
National Gallery of Ireland, Dublin
National Museum, Warsaw
Nationalmuseum, Stockholm
Philadelphia Museum of Art
Private Collection
Private Collection, Boston
Private Collection, France
Private Collection, The Netherlands
Private Collection, New York
Private Collection, Switzerland
Private Collection, United Kingdom
Private Collection, United States
The Putnam Foundation, Timken Museum of Art,
    San Diego
Rijksmuseum, Amsterdam
Royal Cabinet of Paintings, Mauritshuis, The Hague
Sinebrychoff Art Museum, Helsinki
Staatliches Museum, Schwerin
Städelsches Kunstinstitut, Frankfurt am Main
Statens Museum for Kunst, Copenhagen
Szépmüvészeti Múzeum, Budapest (Museum of
    Fine Art, Budapest)

Cat 4, detail

Essays

Love Letters: Dutch Genre Paintings in the Age of Vermeer
Peter C. Sutton

Lors même que nous serions parfois séparés, nous pourrions, par la correspondance, rester présents l'un à l'autre. Au reste, les mots que l'on écrit sont souvent plus hardis que ceux que l'on prononce de la bouche (When we are sometimes separated, we can keep in one another's company through correspondence. Moreover, words that one writes are often more enduring than those that one speaks).
—Abelard to Héloïse, 12th century, France

La voix se perd, l'ecriture demeure (The spoken word is fugitive, the written endures).
—Jan van de Velde, *Lettre defensive, pour l'art de bien escrire* (Rotterdam, 1599)

Jae, al zijn menschen wijdt van een ghevloden / Sy malkander door stomme boden (Though they be far apart, people speak to one another via silent messengers).
—Karel van Mander, *Het Schilderboeck* (Middelburg, 1603), pt. 1, fol. 51b

Het is net als ik praat Song, als ik schrift (It's just as if I were chatting with you, Song, when I write).
—Dorothea van Dorp to Constantijn Huygens, The Hague, 1624

Neem eens, ick kreegh een jonghman lief, / Sal ick niet soetjens, met een brief, / Hem mogen klagen mijnen noot? (If I am fond of a young man, / Should I not take the time at last to express my feelings in a letter / That he might know my longing?).
—Rosette to Sibille, in Jacob Cats, *Houwelick* (Middelburg, 1625)

Letters have been cherished for their intimacy and immediacy throughout the history of Western culture. They have taken many forms and served as many literary functions as there have been authors, from official declarations and public manifestos to poetic tributes, pedestrian factual reports, and, of course, the most private of secrets, confessions, and the impassioned murmurings of lovers. The long and eloquent epistles of the ancient world, codified by Cicero and Horace or the fervent Christian writings that St. Paul and St. Jerome patterned on those classical epistles have endured and inspired through the centuries. The eighteenth century is now often celebrated by the English-speaking world as the Golden Age of letters, since John Dryden, Alexander Pope, and Thomas Jefferson, whose Declaration of Independence is an epistle, helped revive and revitalize this letter form, while Samuel Richardson first published his novels framed and crafted as letters, *Pamela* (1740) and *Clarissa* (1747). However, it was the seventeenth century that witnessed the first true explosion of letter writing in both the public-literary realm and the private world. The *Lettres portugaises* of 1667 by Gabriel Joseph de Lavergne Guilleragues (1628–1685) and the letter novel, however modest, by Edme Boursault (1638–1701), popularly known as *Lettres à Babet* of 1669, are the first true epistolary novels, and they had appeared almost a century earlier than Richardson's acclaimed works.

The sheer volume of letter writing in the seventeenth century can scarcely be exaggerated. The letters of Guez de Balzac (1599–1654), published in Leiden in 1648, run to twenty-seven volumes. One of the greatest Dutch poets, Pieter Cornelisz. Hooft (1581–1647), communicated daily in superbly crafted letters on a vast array of topics—literature, poetry, politics, natural history, the classics, not to mention affairs of the heart—with virtually all the leading Dutch thinkers of his day.[1] Indeed, the history of the Dutch Golden Age can often best be appreciated and recaptured by the eyewitness accounts of professional and personal letters.[2] The secretary to the Prince of Orange in The Hague, Constantijn Huygens (1596–1687), was an early champion of Rembrandt and the recipient of the famous artist's most famous letter.[3] He was portrayed in 1627 by Thomas de Keyser in characteristic fashion handing a letter to a clerk or messenger (*fig. 1*). It is estimated that the indefatigable Huygens penned 78,000 letters in his lifetime. Many of these naturally had to do with affairs of state, politics, and diplomacy, but Huygens also kept up almost daily written correspondence with friends and family (see below), as did an increasingly large segment of the population in the Netherlands.[4] The burgeoning fashion for letter writing demanded a broadcast and efficient postal system, as well as ancillary services and accessories, human and literary, such as professional letter writers and the publication of letter-writing manuals.

Dutch artists were the first to make the letter a central theme in images of everyday life, or what we have come to call genre scenes. Masters like Dirck Hals, Gerard ter Borch, Gabriel Metsu, Frans van Mieris, Jan Steen, Pieter de Hooch, and Johannes Vermeer produced wonderfully memorable images of people reading, writing, receiving, and dispatching letters. These paintings would establish the forms that letter themes took for the next three centuries in art, in England, France, Spain, the United States, and elsewhere throughout the Western world. The body of work by seventeenth-century Dutch genre painters and its inspiration constitute the subject of this exhibition. Our selection of works is deliberately limited to genre scenes (and a select few history paintings in the guise of or related to genre) as opposed to portraits or still lifes, in which letters also appear. In the former, the letter was a time-honored detail, or what in the parlance of portraiture in art history is known as an "attribute," which could advertise the sitter's status as a literate individual, *homo literatus*, or, if an address appeared on the same, identify the person portrayed. Letters in still lifes had, in addition to various important mimetic and illusionistic functions, the capacity, through inscriptions feigning an address or a dedication, to alert the viewer to a variety of ideas, associations, and symbolic messages.[5]

However, the functions of letters in anonymous genre scenes are at once more obscure and more intriguing, depicting a range of public and private needs and practices while intimating a richer world of social and psychological interaction. Letter writing evolved and flourished because it was initially regarded as an extension of social ideals that celebrated letters as written conversation. Genre paintings depicting people with letters in turn became distinct from other forms of figure paintings with letters. Letter themes in genre paintings

run the gamut from matter-of-fact transactions in the offices of lawyers, notaries, or *secretarisen*, to scenes of dictation, sometimes in a military context, with an amanuensis or scribe, to the delivery and reception of letters, the private satisfaction or torment of composition, and the thrill or dashed hopes of the letter received.

Dutch genre paintings document for the first time in any culture the full range and power of letters, not merely as an expression of ritualistic social interaction but as a highly personal form of communication delivering pleasure, pain, and a full spectrum of emotion. Since we rarely can see what is written on the letters in these pictures, we must interpolate their contents from the pictorial context or our understanding of the forms and functions of letters in the society that produced them. For this reason this introduction will cast its net broadly in evoking the social, cultural, and literary history of the time, while reserving a closer reading of the imagery for the individual catalogue entries.[6]

The Birth of the Letter Theme

The earliest genre paintings depicting figures with letters seem to have been executed about 1630 in Haarlem and Amsterdam. Although he is better known

for his multifigured merry company and musical scenes, Dirck Hals, brother and pupil of the famous portraitist Frans Hals, seems to have been the first to depict women reading letters alone in simple interiors, sometimes by candlelight at night (see cat. 1). Painted in a free and simple manner, these works have an unpretentious conception of and expository approach to their subjects, which seems well suited to their candid exploration of an unprecedented theme, namely the range of emotion elicited by the solitary reading of letters. Hals's women express by turns cozy pleasure (cat. 1) and unbuttoned contentment and satisfaction (cat. 2), but also anxiety, as in the painting from Mainz, in which a woman tears up a letter (fig. 2), or pensive reverie, as for example in the painting formerly in the Khanenko Collection, Kiev, where a seated woman holding a letter has kicked off her shoe and stares off inscrutably into space (fig. 3). Hals executed these paintings in the same years that he helped pioneer the painting of domestic themes and scenes of women ministering to small children; thus the letter theme arose in the context of an examination of the private life of women in the home.

The earliest certainly dated letter painting seems to be the picture by the artist in Mainz dated 1631 (fig. 2); however, other works by Hals and those of the painter Pieter Codde, who was active only twelve miles away in Amsterdam, may predate it. (The subject may also have caught on early in Delft as well, since an unattributed painting of a woman writing appeared in an inventory reference in that city as early as 1634.[7]) Codde probably knew the Hals family and in 1637 even finished a group portrait begun by Frans Hals, popularly known as *The Meager Company* (Rijksmuseum, Amsterdam, no. C374). Like Dirck he specialized in small-scale paintings of merry company and guardroom scenes, but when he turned to the letter theme he painted a solitary woman. Codde's painting in a private collection in Boston (cat. 3) depicts an elegantly dressed woman viewed from behind seated at a table with a virginal. Some have assumed that she has been interrupted as she played music, but the way in which she sits, sidesaddle on the chair with arm dangling loose, suggests she sat down suddenly. The sheet of paper she holds is folded several times, as one would a letter, not sheet music. We cannot know her expression or thoughts as she stares silently into the corner, but her heavy form suggests reflection. In a close variant of this picture now in the Rau collection (cat. 3, fig. 1), another elegantly attired woman appears in virtually the same position but in mirror image. The musical instruments are now replaced by a table with candlestick, book, writing supplies, as well as a silver wine beaker, and the woman wears a black veil, suggesting the once tightly folded letter in her hand has brought darker, more unsettling news.

It is surely not a matter of chance that the first paintings to deal with the letter theme explore a range

Fig. 2. Dirck Hals
Woman Tearing up a Letter
Signed and dated: *1631*
Oil on panel, 45 x 55 cm
Landesmuseum, Mainz, no. 168

Fig. 3. Dirck Hals
Woman with a Letter
Oil on panel, 47 x 57 cm
Formerly Khanenko Collection, Kiev

of emotion and emphasize the privacy of letters through their occluded designs, notably the self-absorbed figures viewed from behind. Hals was a member of the local rhetoricians' society, and Codde was an amateur poet involved in literary circles in Amsterdam at the time that he executed these pictures; thus both men appreciated the power of written words to move people. In exploring the private, interior world of letters and their emotions, the two artists were joined in their efforts by another so-called guardroom painter, Willem Duyster. We know that Duyster and Codde had met by 1625, when a document records a quarrel between the two artists. Duyster would die young from plague only a decade later, but his few surviving genre scenes show him to be a master of psychology, whether it is in a scene of soldiers with hostages, merry companies, or a couple with a letter. In Duyster's painting from Copenhagen (cat. 4), another elegantly clad lady in black silk with a broad lace collar has been reading a letter that she holds to her bosom. She seems to have taken it with others that lie open before her on a table from a small black lacquered box. Behind her stands an officer with a sash and slouch hat smiling down over her shoulder, as if to sneak a glimpse of the letter's contents. She offers him no more than a tight-lipped smile and a sidelong glance. Once again we are not privy to the contents of the letters, but they seem not only to be worthy of retaining as keepsakes but also can elicit the curiosity of a third party—a desire that seemingly grew in intensity over the thirty years that separate the present work from Gabriel Metsu's stealthy eavesdropper in his famous so-called *Letter-Writer Surprised* (fig. 12) in the Wallace Collection.

Gerard ter Borch

The artist who first popularized the letter theme and rang the changes most extensively on its richly varied associations was Gerard ter Borch. Born to a distinguished family in Zwolle, Gerard ter Borch was encouraged to draw from a very early age by his father and in 1634 took an apprenticeship in Haarlem, where he would have encountered Dirck Hals's art, and became a master the following year. Although he traveled extensively abroad in his early career, his guardroom scenes from the 1640s are descended from those of native Dutch guardroom painters, like Codde, Duyster, and Anthonie Palamedes. But ter Borch avoided the dramatic action and theatrical emotion associated with the Baroque; from the beginning, his figures have a stillness and interior life that are distinctive.

During the period corresponding to ter Borch's early career, the most innovative stylistic developments and original new subjects in Dutch genre painting were created in Leiden in the circle of Gerard Dou, whose highly refined and detailed *fijnschilder* manner was widely imitated, not only by his foremost pupil, Frans van Mieris (see cats. 21–26), but also by many other independent painters. Although Dou depicted people reading books and preparing to write—for example, sharpening a quill—he did not address the letter theme. However, the subject became a particular favorite among other Leiden painters, not only van Mieris and other Dou followers but also Quirijn van Brekelenkam and Gabriel Metsu.

Ter Borch, by contrast, made letters a centerpiece of his innovative approach to genre painting in the late 1640s and early 1650s. These works were mostly painted

Fig. 4. Gerard ter Borch
Unwelcome News
Monogrammed and dated: *1653*
Oil on panel, 67.7 x 59.5 cm
Royal Cabinet of Paintings,
Mauritshuis, The Hague, no. 176

Fig. 5. Anthonie Palamedes
Guardroom Scene with a Trumpeter Delivering a Message
Oil on panel, 38.7 x 50 cm
Herzog Anton Ulrich-Museum,
Braunschweig, Kunstmuseum
des Landes Niedersachsen,
no. 325

Fig. 6. Gerard ter Borch
Woman Reading a Letter with a Rustic Messenger
Oil on panel, 59 x 48 cm
State Hermitage Museum, Saint Petersburg

Fig. 7. Gerard ter Borch
Letter Reader
Oil on canvas, 44.2 x 32.2 cm
The Wallace Collection, London, no. P236

Fig. 8. Gerard ter Borch
Woman Drinking with a Letter
Oil on canvas, 38.9 x 29.7 cm
Städelsches Kunstinstitut, Frankfurt a. M., no. 1055

in an upright format and depict a few brightly lit, half-
and full-length figures whose placement and gestures,
rather the setting and environment, define the dark
pictorial space. He continued to paint guardroom
subjects, such as the *Unwelcome News*, dated 1653
(*fig. 4*), during these years. These owe a debt to works
from the previous decade by artists like the Delft
painter of soldiers on bivouac, Palamedes (*fig. 5*), but are
infinitely better articulated, not simply in the drawing
of figures but also in their characterization. While both
paintings depict trumpeters delivering a letter with
written orders to an officer, ter Borch adds the officer's
reclining female companion, languid and bored at
his knee, as well as a rich and subtle nonverbal
communication between the two military men,
seemingly fraught with issues of rank, station, and the
inconvenience of marching orders. Ter Borch would
return to the subject of orders received in a painting
executed a few years later now in Dresden (cat. 6),
where once more the trumpeter-messenger remains
respectfully standing, hat in hand, as the officer reads the
letter. Now, however, the figures have a greater clarity
and monumentality.

It was in these same years, the early 1650s, that ter
Borch brought a new elegance to the painting of high-
life genre scenes featuring beautiful ladies in magnificent
satin gowns entertaining themselves or gentlemen callers
in their private apartments. The letter theme proved
perfectly suited to these *tableaux de mode*, or "polite
genre." Yet ter Borch's paintings are more than mere
illustrations of the upper-class social life in Holland that
was increasingly influenced by French manners. They
offer richly suggestive narratives and invite the viewer

into a conspiratorial participation in a mostly feminine world, intimate and leisured. Ter Borch painted as many as sixteen genre scenes involving letters (see as examples cats. 5-10). These are not true narrative cycles but address aspects of the subject that were unprecedented in variety. Ter Borch elevated the letter theme from mere anecdote to the level of poetic meditation and subtle dramatic intrigue. One of his earliest explorations of the theme, the painting from the Hermitage (*fig. 6*), depicts a seated young lady in splendid yellow and white satin and a black headdress contentedly reading a letter. A rustic messenger in a gray coat with staff and letter bag slung over his shoulder awaits her instructions. Beyond the table set with silver platter, candlestick, and ceramic pitcher is a young black serving woman before a pavilion bed, all of which evokes the setting of a well-appointed home.

The perfect embodiment of this elegant new treatment of the letter theme is ter Borch's *Woman Writing a Letter*, of 1655 or later, from the Mauritshuis (cat. 5). This exquisitely memorable little picture is the first depiction ever painted of a woman writing a letter. Her concentration and absorption in her task are complete and mesmerizing. And the care with which the artist has composed his picture—highlighting her form in profile, emphasizing the graceful curve of her neck, and placing the blue ribbon from which her pearl earring hangs at the very center of the design—is masterfully conceived and enchanting in its timeless balance. Although ter Borch would execute many other paintings on the subject, this work and the single *Letter Reader* (*fig. 7*), painted a few years later and now in the Wallace Collection, London, epitomize the intimacy and motionless contemplation of the subject. Other single-figure images of ladies with letters by ter Borch suggest that the unseen contents of the letter might prompt a smile, but just as readily require the recipient to fortify herself with a drink (*fig. 8* and cat. 10). And in one subdued painting (*fig. 9*), the young woman's black widow's weeds leave little doubt that the letter is a notification of death or a condolence letter.

Although their companionship was long overlooked because of a misreading of dimensions of one of the works, ter Borch's two paintings from the Philadelphia Museum of Art and a private collection that are here reunited (cats. 8 & 9) are probably also the first pendants to address the theme of a man writing a letter and a woman responding.[8] In the first, an officer writes a letter as a trumpeter waits to deliver it; in the second, a woman seals a letter to be delivered by a serving woman holding a marketing pail. The quiet patience of the two messengers confers a solemnity on and helps pique our interest in the otherwise uneventful activity of writing

Fig. 9. Gerard ter Borch
Woman in Mourning Clothes Reading a Letter
Oil on canvas, 44 x 39 cm
Private Collection

a letter. The two works have complementary designs as well as themes, juxtaposing similar settings and furnishings, comparable figures (the postillion and the maidservant), even contrasting details such as the dogs (a hound suitable to a male world and a daintier lapdog for the feminine interior). The ace of hearts playing card on the floor of the Philadelphia painting suggests that the officer addresses his lady from the heart. As Otto Naumann first observed, Dirck Hals's paintings in Mainz and formerly in Kiev (*figs. 2 & 3*) may have been the first pendants dealing with letters. But ter Borch's pendants would inspire generations of companion pieces linking lovers though perhaps none as successfully as those of Gabriel Metsu (see cats. 16 & 17, and 18 & 19). The companionship of these several pendants highlights the dialogue implicit in the letter theme of correspondence and underscores the romantic associations so often aroused by the subject.

Ter Borch's exploration of the letter theme was not restricted to the lone writer or recipient, or even to the two principal correspondents, but became a social event, albeit in the rarified sorority of highborn women in their boudoirs—in the type of picture that the great nineteenth-century connoisseur, John Smith, called the

Fig. 10. Gerard ter Borch
The Letter
Oil on canvas, 79.5 x 68 cm
Her Majesty the Queen, Buckingham Palace, London, no. 1406

Fig. 11. Gerard ter Borch
Curiosity
Oil on canvas, 76.2 x 62.2 cm
The Metropolitan Museum of Art, New York, acc. no. 49.7.38

artist's "fancy compositions." [9] The artist's painting in Buckingham Palace (*fig. 10*) depicts a standing lady in a ravishing silk gown reading a letter, possibly out loud, which presumably has been composed by another no less elegantly attired lady in a fur-trimmed jacket seated at a writing desk with paper. A serving boy with basin and ewer stands at the back, seemingly lost in a moment of forgetfulness and awe, slack-jawed to be in the presence of two such exquisite creatures in an intimate moment. And in the painting known by the apocryphal title *Curiosity*, in the Metropolitan Museum of Art, New York (*fig. 11*), the contents of the letter are so intriguing that the letter writer's woman friend strains up on the chair back precariously to peer over her shoulder to read its contents, while a third standing lady in silk looks directly out from the picture, acknowledging us and in so doing bringing us into this charmed circle of friends. Even the lapdog seems fascinated by the letter's contents. Gabriel Metsu's *The Letter-Writer Surprised* (*fig. 12*) repeats the motif of the figure looking over the woman's shoulder as she writes (indeed even adds a bust that seems comically to do the same, looking down with curiosity at the letter from atop a chest behind); but by substituting a man for

a female companion, Metsu introduces an intruder into this sanctuary of female privacy, threatening the precious confidentiality of the letter.

Ter Borch's pupil Caspar Netscher certainly knew and was influenced by his teacher's letter paintings; he even posed for the figure of the officer in ter Borch's letter paintings in Philadelphia (cat. 8) and London (cat. 8, *fig. 1*). However, Netscher made his own original contributions to the subject, painting, for example, a wistfully thoughtful man seated writing a letter with chin in hand staring off into space (cat. 11). Whereas ter Borch invented the subject of the woman writing (cat. 5) and depicted military men writing, they are never alone, always attended by other soldiers with whom they sometimes seem to consult or to whom they dictate. Netscher is exceptional, therefore, in depicting a solitary man composing a letter. With head in hand, the writer assumes the traditional pose of Melancholia, as would a more dejected-looking young lady with a letter in a painting by Netscher formerly with Jack Kilgore (*fig. 13*). If ter Borch was the master of understated gestures expressing internalized feeling, Netscher explored more outward, even theatrical approaches to narration, painting for example *The Letter with the Black Seal* (cat. 12), in which a young woman with hands aflutter makes a dramatic rhetorical gesture of alarm as she receives what no doubt is word of a death from a tearful maidservant. Her counterpart in happy contentment is the smiling young woman who holds her beloved's medallion as she looks out at the viewer with evident satisfaction in Netscher's painting from Kassel (cat. 13).

Gabriel Metsu

One of the most accomplished masters of the letter theme was Gabriel Metsu, to whose colorful, elegantly soigné, and graceful art it seemed ideally suited. Metsu painted a *huisvrouw* who had set her sewing aside to quietly enjoy a letter (cat. 15), as well as a chicly attired lady who, like Vermeer's letter writer in the painting from Washington (cat. 38), interrupts her writing to smile and look directly and confidently out at the viewer, quill poised like a director's baton (cat. 20). However, he was at his best when treating the theme with the eloquent dialogue of companion pieces. Metsu painted several pairs of paintings, including his self-portrait with his wife in pendant portraits in the J. B. Speed Art Museum, Louisville (see cat. 16, *figs. 1, 2*), two market scenes of 1662 preserved in the Gemäldegalerie, Dresden (inv. nos. 1733, 1734), and a pair of genre scenes in the Musée du Louvre (inv. nos. 1464, 1465), which juxtapose a woman drinking and smoking and a woman peeling apples in a kitchen, evidently as a moral admonition about idleness and industry—the grasshopper and the ant, as it were, of domesticity. When he turned to the letter theme it was surely not a matter of accident that he chose more elegant, upscale settings. In the painting in Montpellier (cat. 16) the gentleman in a long, fancy coat sits writing a letter in a book-lined study at a table with a costly oriental carpet as a serving woman approaches with a lighted candle. In the companion piece, the woman is again seated at a table, but beneath a loggia, a garden and stately home in the distance, an urn of flowers on the table. She has covered her head and shoulders against the fresh breeze and interrupts her reading of the book that rests in her lap to receive a letter from a boy who doffs his hat deferentially. The man and woman are separated by an imagined distance but linked by the letter and the paintings' complementary three-quarter-length designs, in which they face one another as if in unspoken conversation.

The greatest pair of letter paintings is the companion pieces by Metsu in the National Gallery of Ireland (cats. 18 & 19). These postdate by at least a half dozen years the pair in San Diego and Montpellier that probably date from the late 1650s. They adopt a more colorful palette, a brighter, silvery tonality, and subtler, more sophisticated,

Fig. 12. Gabriel Metsu
The Letter Writer Surprised, c. 1660
Oil on panel, 45.2 x 38.6 cm
The Wallace Collection, London, no. P240

Fig. 13. Caspar Netscher
Woman with a Letter
Oil on canvas, 73.5 x 59.5 cm
Private Collection, United States

full-length designs. The man again sits writing at a table covered with a carpet but now is situated before an open window admitting a cool daylight. He turns away from the woman to whom he presumably writes, as if to emphasize his remove, but she too sits by the light of a window as she reads a letter, inclining her head prettily in his direction. Both rooms have tiled floors, in his case of expensive imported black and white marble set in diamond-shaped patterns, and bright whitewashed walls hung with paintings. At the back of the woman's scene stands a maidservant supporting a pail on her hip and holding another letter in her hand. She raises a curtain to examine a blustery seascape, which again suggests the distance that separates the correspondents. Although she sits in an attitude of classic composure, embodying an ideal of serene domesticity, the woman apparently was excited enough by the arrival of the letter that she not only set aside her sewing but dropped her thimble, which now lies neglected on the floor at the lower right.

The Delft School: Pieter de Hooch and Johannes Vermeer

Part of the success and beauty of Metsu's pendants is their expressive use of space, which probably is indebted to Delft School painting and the art of Pieter de Hooch and Johannes Vermeer. In the mid-1650s and certainly by 1658, de Hooch had mastered a command of both linear and aerial perspective that was unprecedented among genre painters. No earlier artist had depicted interior and courtyard spaces with such naturalism. De Hooch was the first to fully appreciate that the illusion of space is not merely a matter of orthogonals, or lines of sight, converging in a vanishing point but also a product of light, color, and atmosphere. He had addressed the letter theme in his early guardroom scenes (specifically, *Unwelcome News*, Cambó Collection, Barcelona, which is based on ter Borch's painting of the same theme in the Mauritshuis, *fig. 4*) but did not take it up again until after he had left Delft in about 1660–61 for burgeoning Amsterdam. It was in that wealthy and magnetic city that he began to address more elegant subjects in upper-class settings, once again chiefly under the influence of ter Borch. However, unlike ter Borch, who never offers a view to an adjoining room, let alone a prospect to the out-of-doors, de Hooch coupled the letter theme with an expressive use of the geometry of architecture to convey the notion of private and public thresholds and boundaries crossed by private correspondence. In de Hooch's art, letters connect the domestic realm, above all of women, with a wider public world viewed through doorways and windows.

Early in de Hooch's years in Amsterdam he depicted a women silently reading a letter by a window with a view of the city's skyline in the distance (cat. 34). Somewhat later he painted what is no doubt an imaginary interior with a very elegantly dressed lady reading a letter as a messenger relaxes with a glass of wine, leaning on an open windowsill (cat. 35). As she concentrates on her reading, the messenger casually awaits her response, staring off into the distance through the window, ever the itinerant and restive figure of the road, while the maidservant, by contrast, is the perennial inhabitant of the home; her silent and closed form, hands clasped before her, hovers silently in the shadows. Beyond her, through the open doorway, is a lighter and airier world of privilege symbolized by the facade of a sunlit mansion. In another painting by de Hooch, a man seems to read a letter aloud to a woman who has put aside her needlework to listen, leaning slightly as if to cock her ear to the recitation (cat. 37). And one of de Hooch's finest mature paintings is the image dated 1670 in the Rijksmuseum (cat. 36) of a seated woman holding a letter in one hand and pointing with the other to the open door, seemingly instructing a young messenger holding a letter aloft about its recipient and destination. Like Metsu's letter reader (cat. 19), she sits on a little raised platform, or *soldertje*, that had the dual purpose of lifting her off the cold stone floor and enabling her to make use of the light of the window for needlework and reading. In de Hooch's art, light is always a cheering, optimistic element in a tenebrous world. The doorway and wall of backlighted windows open onto the Keiszersgracht in Amsterdam. Light enters *contre-jour* through the orderly scrim—the porous membrane of the facade of the canal house—softly illuminating the scene and dispersing over the marble floor, becoming a metaphor for the openness to the wider world facilitated by letters.

Six of Vermeer's rare paintings, or nearly one-fifth of his *oeuvre*, are dedicated to the letter theme and are discussed in an essay in this volume by Lisa Vergara. Vermeer brought the letter subject to classical perfection, transmuting the merely incidental and anecdotal into timelessly memorable images—poised, opalescent, and so sublimely balanced as to seem inevitable. Once again his world of letters is a feminine one, with women standing in the light reading letters alone with such hushed expectation that they seem to hold their breath (see Vergara, *figs. 52, 54*) or calmly looking out at us with disarming candor as they compose (cat. 38). Here, too, we encounter the silent but essential and sometimes charged dialogue between the lady and her maidservant as letters come and go (see cat. 39 and *figs. 57, 58*), creating subtle dramas that linger unresolved within a world governed by codes of domestic conduct. As with de Hooch's interiors, the organization of the space and the distribution of the light are essential components of these narratives. But whereas de Hooch's account of the upper-middle-class world that supported the new fashion for letters is prosaic in the best sense of the word—naturalistic, expository, and compellingly descriptive—Vermeer elevates the subject to a more sublime and generalized realm, a resonant and poetic world, the evocation and analysis of which has inspired generations of wordsmiths.

Adriaen van Ostade

While ter Borch, Metsu, the Delft artists, and most genre painters reserved the letter theme for high-life scenes, the renowned peasant painter Adriaen van Ostade depicted the lower classes reading letters, lending some credence to foreign observers' reports of widespread literacy in seventeenth-century Holland (*fig. 14*). His small painting in the Musée du Louvre depicts a smiling man in a window holding a letter in one hand and spectacles in the other (*fig. 15*) and may be a personification of Sight in a series of the Five Senses; it has a pendant (Musée du Louvre, inv. M.I. 943) depicting a drinker (possibly Taste from an incomplete series). Ostade also depicted figures reading in taverns (see, for example, Musée du Louvre, inv. M.I. 946, dated 1653), some of whom, for example, the gentleman in the black cap and sleeveless tabard who reads a letter or document in the painting dated 1655 in Allentown (*fig. 16*), seem to be rural lawyers or possibly notaries. In the latter picture, the little still life on the table includes the reader's spectacle case, while overhead on the wall hangs a doodlesack—a musical instrument like a bagpipes that was notoriously associated with fools, thus possibly functioning as an admonition in this context. Beginning at least with Pieter Brueghel the Younger and probably with his father, the great originator of peasant themes, lawyers were pilloried in sixteenth- and seventeenth-century art as overpriced professionals who preyed on the illiterate peasantry. Pieter de Bloot and Cornelis Saftleven were among earlier seventeenth-century Dutch artists who painted lawyers' offices with peasants at the mercy of their advocates; the latter even satirized them with animal parodies, illustrating in one such picture in Rotterdam (Boijmans-van Beuningen Museum, inv. 1768) the saying inscribed on the picture: "die wille rechten / om een koe / die brengter / noch een toe" (He who sues over a cow, will pay with another).

Yet when Adriaen van Ostade returned to the theme of a lawyer with a letter or document about 1668, he treated the lawyer as a respectable and studious professional without any hint of criticism (see cats. 28, 29 & 30). It has often been observed that Ostade's peasants became tamer and more domesticated after he married a

Fig. 14. Adriaen van Ostade
Peasant Reading a Letter
Signed and dated: *1668*
Oil on panel, 23.5 x 18.7 cm
Private Collection (on loan to Wallraf Richartz Museum, Cologne), inv. no. Dep. 564

Fig. 15. Adriaen van Ostade
Man with a Letter at a Window
Oil on panel, 27 x 22 cm
Musée du Louvre, Paris, inv. M.I. 944

Fig. 16. Adriaen van Ostade
Man Reading in a Tavern (The Village Lawyer)
Signed and dated: *1655*
Oil on panel, 37.1 x 29.8 cm
Allentown Art Museum, Samuel H. Kress Collection, 1961
(1961.48)

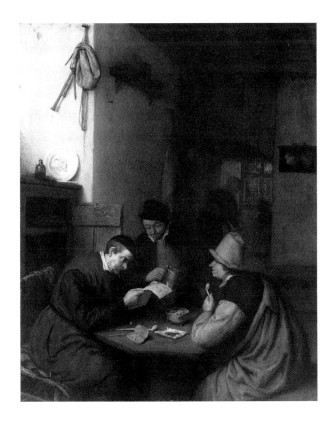

Fig. 17. Michiel van Musscher (after Cornelis Dusart?)
Lawyer with a Peasant Client
Signed and dated: *1668*
Oil on canvas, 45 x 40 cm
Formerly Van Aelst Collection, Hoevelaken

Fig. 18. Job Berckheyde
Lawyer or Notary in His Office with a Peasant Client
Signed and dated: *1672*
Oil on canvas, 78.5 x 62.2 cm
Sale, Christie's, London, April 22, 1994, no. 12 (as M. van
Musscher)

Fig. 19. Ludolph de Jongh
Messenger Reading a Letter in a Tavern
Signed and dated: *1657*
Oil on canvas, 65 x 53 cm
Landesmuseum, Mainz, inv. no. 800

wealthy Catholic woman in 1657 and presumably moved up in the world. Whether this softened his perception of lawyers and other professionals is unknown, but he seems to have painted more than one dozen images of lawyers in his later career. In the work of Ostade's pupil Cornelis Dusart and Michiel van Musscher, lawyers are again caricatured as rapacious abusers of the peasantry (*fig. 17*). And even in Job Berckheyde's painting of a lawyer or possibly a notary handing a paper to a peasant client (*fig. 18*), the smirking assistant who laughs at the fumbling old man descends from the pictorial tradition of arrogant advocates.

The subject of a figure reading a letter, probably aloud, in a tavern to a group of customers and wait staff was taken up by the Rotterdam genre painter Ludolph de Jongh, in a painting of 1657 in Mainz (*fig. 19*). The seated man on the left undoubtedly is the postal courier, identified by the long horn hanging at his back. The two old men and standing serving girl in an apron seem to hang on his every word, no doubt because they cannot read themselves. But in de Jongh's painting of about 1665 in Ascott House (*fig. 20*), the letter arrives in a much grander interior, the *voorhuis* of a house decorated with marble floor, gilt-leather wall coverings, and a large

history painting in a gold frame, delivered, not by a rustic courier, but by a page in extravagant livery, red cape, tights, open-mouthed boots, and sword. Even the frisking dogs seem to convey carefree aristocratic insouciance and the spirit of *dolce far niente*. De Jongh's theme of a letter read aloud was treated in what may be a theatrical context in an airier setting by the Amsterdam genre painter Gerard van Zijl (*fig. 21*), who depicts an elegantly clad lady reading to a group of contemporaries. Here the richly costumed listeners presumably could read for themselves, but to judge from their rapt expressions, they are spellbound by the lady's recitation.

Frans van Mieris and Later Fijnschilders

The Leiden *fijnschilder* Frans van Mieris painted six letter paintings, three of which are nocturnal scenes (see cats. 20–22); most date from his later career, about 1670–81. These showcase the highly enameled touch and deeply saturated hues that the artist favored in his last years. The earliest dated example is a more delicately nuanced night scene of 1667 (cat. 21) depicting a lady in a lovely red velvet and white fur–trimmed jacket and linen headdress sealing a letter as a serving boy waits to one side and a second woman in the background is just

Fig. 20. Ludolph de Jongh
Woman Receiving a Letter, c. 1665
Oil on canvas, 58.5 x 72.5 cm
Ascott House (National Trust), Buckinghamshire

Fig. 21. Gerard van Zijl
Woman Reading a Letter Aloud
Oil on canvas, 30.4 x 25.7 cm
Butôt Collection

visible bringing another candle. Inconspicuous on the angled writing desk with quill and inkstand on the left is the scissoring outline of an opened letter—no doubt the missive to which the lady responds. The painting's impeccable finish speaks to the refinement of the social activity that inspired its subject. Newly reemerged, the work is fully signed and dated and is now recognized as the original. It owes debts to both Gerard ter Borch in its subject matter (compare cat. 9) and to van Mieris's teacher, Dou, in its nocturnal effects.

Van Mieris was a particularly creative enthusiast of the letter theme, treating it in both paintings and drawings. A charming little picture of 1670 depicts a troubled young lady in an ample beret with head in hand, evidently suffering from writer's block (cat. 22), while another similar half-length work of about the same period depicts the happy letter writer in the full flow of composition (cat. 23). The latter was probably inspired by ter Borch's *Letter Writer* in the Mauritshuis (cat. 5), as clearly was van Mieris's painting of 1680 in the Rijksmuseum (cat. 24). Another newly discovered work, also dated 1680, represents a young lady with a lapdog and an open letter on a table hearkening to an old crone who chatters in her ear, no doubt about the missive's

contents (cat. 26). To its possible subject we will return.

The later *fijnschilder* painters adapted the letter theme in various, sometimes original ways. Eglon van der Neer executed a slickly crafted painting of a standing woman before a mirror (*fig. 22*). Like so many later seventeenth-century Dutch paintings, it is shamelessly lifted from ter Borch's ladies in satin and establishes an astonishing level of technical virtuosity, but typically drains the theme of its richness of personal psychological association, leaving an exercise in costume and manners. Michiel van Musscher, who studied with Metsu, obviously was well acquainted with ter Borch's art, basing his own *Woman Reading a Letter* of 1670 (cat. 14) on two of the master's paintings. Among other interesting examples among the later *fijnschilders* is Godfried Schalcken's little image of an unusual subject, an old man evidently writing as he reads a letter or sheet of paper, possibly taking notes or transcribing the contents (*fig. 23*). The old gent conforms to the scholar types that Dou popularized, but rather than consulting a book he scrutinizes a letter. Carel de Moor depicted an abundantly upholstered lady placing a dainty forefinger to her lip in a cloyingly studied pose of concentration (cat. 22, *fig. 1*). And as the settings of Dutch genre scenes became ever grander under the

25

Fig. 22. Eglon van der Neer
Woman Reading a Letter with a Maid Servant
Oil on canvas, 81 x 66 cm
Private Collection

Fig. 23. Godfried Schalcken
Old Man Reading a Letter while Writing
Oil on panel, 12 x 9 cm
Musée du Louvre, Paris, inv. 1832

influence of the French, Frans's son, Willem van Mieris, in 1680 depicted a lady reading a letter in an elaborately columned space beside two lavishly attired gentlemen in long robes playing tric-trac (cat. 43). In Dutch, the game, *verkeerspel*, literally means "game of changes." The officer and his lady friend in the masterpiece by the Delft painter Johannes Verkolje in the Mauritshuis (cat. 42) also play tric-trac as the trumpeter rushes in, no doubt disturbing their peaceful recreation with marching orders. The power of letters to bring sudden changes of fortune surely explains why they were coupled with the game. One last painting by Johannes's son, Nicholaes Verkolje (cat. 42), demonstrates that Gerard Dou's polished fijnschilder style as well as his nocturnal "niche" compositions continued to inspire followers well into the eighteenth century. Here the young lady accompanied by a maidservant accomplice holds a letter and a candle as she gestures encouragingly to an unseen suitor below from her window.

Liberty and Literacy

The letter became a clearly established theme in Dutch genre painting over the course of the seventeenth century. In many regards the popularity of the subject reflected social and political developments. At the turn of the seventeenth century, the Protestant Republic of the Netherlands had only recently seceded from the Catholic Spanish Netherlands and was embroiled in the Eighty Years' War—the longest in modern history—for their independence. By their perseverance, maritime expertise, and business acumen, the Dutch became the center of a far-flung trading empire and, notwithstanding their diminutive size and the perennial threat of inundation, a major player on the European stage. With their gift for commerce, reputation for tolerance, and receptivity to talented immigrants, the Netherlands saw their populations grow at a time when most of Europe's stagnated or declined. The Dutch soon became not only numerous but also the richest people per capita in all of Christendom and indeed would remain so throughout the eighteenth century. They built great cities, but none was grander or faster growing than Amsterdam, which reigned as the banking capital of northern Europe, the center of the lucrative European grain trade, and an unrivalled emporium for foreign goods.

By the depressed standards of the times, the Dutch also enjoyed a high if not the highest rate of literacy in Europe. Sixteenth-century foreign observers like L. Guicciardini reported that a surprisingly large segment of the population could read.[10] And Scaliger (1540–1609) even remarked that some peasants and serving girls could write, a still higher achievement.[11] As a test of this type of anecdotal information, modern historians have tried to

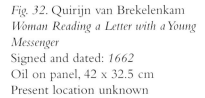

Fig. 31. Quirijn van Brekelenkam
Woman Reading a Letter with a Rustic
Courier Seated
Oil on panel, 45 x 63 cm
Present location unknown

Fig. 32. Quirijn van Brekelenkam
Woman Reading a Letter with a Young
Messenger
Signed and dated: *1662*
Oil on panel, 42 x 32.5 cm
Present location unknown

Fig. 33. Quirijn van Brekelenkam
Man Reading a Letter with a Young Messenger
Signed and dated: *1661*
Oil on panel, 46.8 x 61.8 cm
Hamburger Kunsthalle, inv. 20

connections to the German states and employed *bryffjongen* (literally, "letter youths"), who wore outfits of blue "English" cloth.[24] The early *stadsboden* carried a silver canister (*bodebus*) that held the letters and wore a messenger's badge carrying the coat of arms of the city for which he worked.[25] When mounted service became the common practice in the Netherlands in the latter half of the seventeenth century, the *posthorn* became the mailman's symbol, which he would sound on arrival and departure, always entering the times in his log book (a curled *posthorn* lies on the floor in the foreground of figure 27). When the volume of letters became too great for the *bodebus*, it was replaced by a large leather rider's valise in which the intercity mail was carried, while a separate compartment with a flap was used for mail picked up and delivered en route (known as the *tussen-post*). There seems not to have been a standard civilian municipal mail deliverer's uniform in the mid–seventeenth century, although the long, blue, caped outfit worn by two messengers depicted by Pieter de Hooch (see cats. 35 and cat. 35, *fig. 1*) suggests there may have been some standardization in messengers' attire.

Clearly, the rustic letter carriers one sees in works by ter Borch awaiting a response (*figs. 6 & 30*) or who rest heavily from their travels in a work by Quirijn van Brekelenkam (*fig. 31*) suggest that rural letter carriers had

little to distinguish them from their fellow travelers. Unlike in great cities like Vienna, Paris, and London, there was no established postal service providing local, street-to-street delivery within Dutch cities. Even mighty Amsterdam was small enough that the delivery of letters across town was entrusted to family members, private courier services, maidservants, or even young boys. This was surely the case in Leiden as well, to judge once again from the several paintings that Brekelekam executed of letter recipients with messengers (*fig. 32*). The elegantly dressed young man who looks out at the viewer and strikes a pose in high boots, his broad hat on his hip, and a sword at his waist as he awaits the gentleman's answer to the letter in Brekelekam's painting in Hamburg (*fig. 33*) suggests a member of a well-to-do household, as does the young messenger in de Hooch's painting in Amsterdam (cat. 36). Guides to the art of courtship recommended using servants as go-betweens, especially for the delivery of letters.[26]

In the Middle Ages, letters were sometimes placed in cloth or woolen envelopes; paper envelopes only appeared in the fifteenth century, albeit rarely, while most letters were simply folded and sealed.[27] Various colored waxes were used—red, green, yellow, and white. Ink also came in different colors, most commonly black, brown, red, or green; even invisible ink was available.[28] Dutch

31

paper was highly regarded, and some fashionable letters were written on stationery with gold borders or perfumed paper. Gerbrand Adriaensz. Bredero's plays often feature love letters; in his *Schijn-heyligh* (The Hypocrite) of 1624, Eelhart orders a mixture of civet and amber to perfume his missive. Quill pens were the most common writing instrument, but reed pens were still in use. Some letters were also tied up with a little cord. Stamps were not introduced until about 1840, but postage seals were commonly employed in the seventeenth century and can be seen being applied by one of the Twant sons in figure 27.

We can appreciate something of the excitement and sense of connection with the wider world that the receipt of private letters evoked in Dutchmen in the seventeenth century from a poem by P. Hondius.

> *De packetten groot en cleen*
> *Stellen, die van elck en een,*
> *Van de vrienden, t'aller stonden,*
> *Dach op dach op zijn geronden.*
> *En hier laet ick alle dagen*
> *Licht een ure stille staen,*
> *Om met lust en welbehagen*
> *Al mijn brieven gae te slaen;*
> *Die mij levert al gelijck*
> *Het geheele Christenrijck:*
> *En van Westen en van Oosten,*
> *In mijn eenheyt comen troosten.*
> *Hondert Heeren aen mij schrijven,*
> *Eer het jaer ten eynde gaet. . . .*
> *Dach op dach, comt mij ter hant*
> *Groot besouck van binnen lant;*
> *En van buyten t'aller wegen*
> *Die met brieven mij bejegen.*
>
> *(Parcels arrive in sets, large and small,*
> *From longtime friends*
> *Day after day they are sent.*
> *And here every day,*
> *All activity comes to a standstill*
> *As I regard my letters*
> *With delight and pleasure*
> *They prove that I am right,*
> *All of Christendom*
> *From the West and from the East.*
> *My correspondence consoles me in my solitude.*
> *One hundred gentlemen will write to me*
> *Before the year is out. . . .*
> *Each day I receive*
> *Many domestic visits*
> *And letters from people far away*
> *Keep me in contact.)*[29]

Letters as Conversation in Polite Society

Letters had long been carriers of public proclamations, instructions, entreaties, dry news and factual information, diplomatic secrets and commercial orders. However, in the latter half of the sixteenth and the seventeenth centuries the notion that letters could also convey private feelings and emotions gradually captured the popular imagination. The writing of private letters had previously been a pastime and token of the upper classes, especially in France, where the practice of writing personal letters was first refined and codified. The ability to compose a good letter was likened to the mastery of the art of conversation and became one of a series of prerequisites for admission to refined, upper-class society.[30] Letter writing was a sign of civility and sociability. To ensure that their sons learned the benefits, techniques, and proper forms of epistolary expression, courtiers, *petits seigneurs*, and self-styled aspirants to erudition retained the services of *secrétaires*. These tutor-secretaries offered everything from practical instruction in how to sharpen a quill pen, mix ink, fold a letter, and master the desired calligraphy (see Ann Adams's essay in this volume), to the proper modes of address, as well as advice on the composition of various types of letters.

A representative of these minor pedagogues was Jean Lemoyne, who produced one of the first letter-writing manuals in about 1550, the title of which captures its practical approach: *L'Instruction de bien et parfaitement écrire, tailler la plume, et autres secrets pour se gouverner en l'art d'écriture, avec quatrains moraux mis par ordre alphabetique pour servir d'exemples aux maîtres exerçant ledit art. . . . Ensemble la copie de plusieurs letters missives* (Instruction in how to write well and perfectly, sharpen the pen, and other secrets to master the art of writing, with moral quatrains placed in alphabetical order to serve as examples for masters practicing the art of editing . . . together with copies of numerous letters). A more influential publication at the outset of the tradition of the letter manual was *Lettres missives et familières* (first published in 1569 and subsequently appearing in thirty editions over the next fifteen years), by Etienne du Tronchet. Du Tronchet was trained as a calligrapher and worked as an administrator for several powerful lords, eventually becoming the secretary to the Queen Mother, Catherine de Médicis. He did not have the literary aspirations of Etienne Pasquier, who was a historian, a cultivated man of letters, and renowned personal stylist, whose *Lettres*, first published in 1586 (and reissued in five editions), sought to legitimize letters written in vernacular French as a literary form. However, du Tronchet's practical approach to letter models won him many followers. Like his successors, he divided his volume into two sections, the first offering general precepts on letter writing and the second offering illustrative examples of a variety of types of letters for different social situations. Written as they were by a scrvant of courtiers, these prescribe the technical constraints imposed by the laws of civility. It is important to recall that the sixteenth century was an age of discretion, when to write down one's true mind was to risk everything. Du Tronchet stressed the importance of these letters as models to be imitated and copied. The volume also included a sampling of love letters, which, like those later published in his *Lettres amoureuses, avec septante sonnets traduits du divin Pétraque* (Paris, 1575), translate or draw extensively on earlier sixteenth-century Italian authors (Bembo, Aretino, Tasso, Caro, Parabosco, etc.). It was usually through the French that the Dutch absorbed Italian literary traditions.

From these followed the publication of a large number of French letter manuals that were read not only in France but also in Holland, where the upper classes, especially as the seventeenth century progressed, took a keen interest in French culture, manners, and literature.[31] None of these manuals proved so popular as Jean Puget de la Serre's *Le Secrétaire à la mode* (1630; see Adams essay, *fig. 66*). Reprinted in at least thirty editions, it was reissued in Amsterdam alone nineteen times between 1643 and 1664, and was translated into Dutch as *Fatsoenlicke zend-brief-schryver* (1651). It offered exemplary letters to fit a wide range of social situations, some of which were real and attributed to their authors, while others were fictitious and unattributed. The author stressed that these should be studied and adapted to the writer's needs, further explaining in his "Instruction à écrire des letters" that there were two types of letters, *lettres d'affaires*, or *Handel-brieven* (business letters), and *lettres de compliment*, or *Brieven van Gedienst-reden of Complimenten* (complimentary letters). The former offer advice or counsel, remonstrate with equals, make fawning entreaties to a superior ("persons of Eminent Quality"), requesting, for example, employment or protection, or recommend some action or offer assistance. The *lettres d'affaires* can also register complaints, assail those who make "backbiting speeches," counter false reports, and even provide exemplary letters offering excuses and ways to solicit pardon for one's own faults. Most are composed in a highly rhetorical style but range in tone from abject pleading and groveling solicitude to stinging contempt and fierce threats. The variety of the *lettres de compliment* is equally rich, offering letters to facilitate a visit, congratulate someone on a marriage, award, or honor, and, in the largest group in this section of the book, letters offering condolences or expressions of gratitude. The consoling letters offer tailored condolences to widows, widowers, and persons who have lost a parent or a child, serving to remind us of how fleeting life could be in the seventeenth century. The "Letter to a Lady who has lost her Husband" (see cat. 12 and fig. 9), here quoted

from the English edition of 1640, captures something of the period's high sentence and gives us a feeling for the rhetoric and sentiment of these models:

> *Madam, Having given you a thousand Testimonies of the particular esteem I made of your Husband, I hope you will not now doubt of the Resentment which remaines to me for his Losse. . . . If I am capable of giving Consolation, I would begin with my selfe, being sensibly touched with the same affliction which torments you. But I leave that care to your Judgement and Vertue, considering that the strength of the one will supply my weaknesse, and the precepts of the other will exceed all the Counsell and Advice that I can impart to you.*

We also sample the chilling stoicism and Christian resignation that high mortality rates demanded in the "Letter from a Husband to his Wife, comforting her upon the Death of their Son":

> *. . . after you have shed some teares, which the Quality of Mother will constraine to you; you must adore (in drying them up) the Omnipotency of him that gave the blow. . . . since God has ordained us to this affliction, we ought to witness by the Moderation of our Complaints, that there is no excesse in his Chastisement.*

Clearly, the letter manuals of the period offer much more than stock solutions to writer's block; they provide a manual of conduct and civility (literally, "lessons of courtship and civility" as the translator's preface puts it in the *Secrétaire à la mode*), enabling an individual to address what were then regarded as virtually all of life's challenges and relationships, with tact, courtesy, and pliant affability—in short, a blueprint for *politesse* and admission to courtly society. It is little wonder that these manuals proved to be best-sellers and that letters were considered so important.

Trained in the classical tradition, Puget de la Serre and Paul Jacob, whose letter manual was entitled *Le Parfait Secrétaire* (Paris, 1656), believed that all epistolary discourse should be based on classical rhetoric, that is, on Cicero's parts of speech. Both writers also stress that letters are a form of dialogue or polite conversation. Jacob likens letters to conversation and emphasizes the importance of knowing the person to whom one is writing, and by implication his or her station in life and expectations: "L'essai d'une bonne letter ou d'un bon discours est de bien connaître les personnes à qui on écrit, et leur préparer toujours ce qui leur est plus proper" (The goal of a good letter or good conversation is to know to whom one writes, and to always be prepared to address them in a manner that is most proper.)[32] Like other letter-manual authors, he emphasizes the importance of adjusting one's rhetorical formulae, especially in the greetings at the beginning and the concluding expressions of sincerity and humility, but also tailoring one's voice and tone to the recipient to establish a social rapport. Puget de la Serre stressed in his description of the *lettre de résponse* the importance of answering each point made by the author of a letter that one has received, creating as it were the mirror image of the prose message to which one responds. The implication is that this creates a written conversation and sustains the mutual respect, balanced exchange, and dialogue that make up the fabric of polite society. The

Fig. 34. Secretaris with a Client
Title page, from D. Mostaert's *Vermeerderde Nederduytsche Secretaris oft zendtbrief schryver* (Amsterdam, 1656)
Koninklijke Bibliotheek, The Hague (28 B 42 titdp.)

importance of complementariness and reciprocity in actual letters has obvious implications for the pendants or companion paintings (see cats. 8 & 9, 16 & 17, 18 & 19) that Dutch painters executed of men writing and women reading letters.

Popular Dutch Letter Manuals

Between 1548 and 1800 there were 19 different letter manuals published in Dutch in 79 editions, which was many fewer than the 230 editions that were published in English during approximately the same period, but a significant literature nonetheless.[33] Among the more popular was Heyman Jacobi's *Ghemeene Seyndtbrieven* (Amsterdam, 1597), the promotional subtitle of which (*seer profijtelijk voor de ouders / meesters en kinderen / om te leeren brieven dichten / ende oock wel te leven / ende ordentlijck te schrijven*) stressed that his instruction offered models not only for writing but also for living. However, the most popular letter-writing manual in Dutch was Daniel Mostaert's *Nederduytsche Secretaris of Zendbriefschrijver*, first published in Amsterdam in 1635 and subsequently appearing in numerous editions.[34] A handy, pocket-sized book, it offered an eminently practical approach to letter writing, advising its aspiring writers in words that still ring true today, "Een Secretaris wordt bequaem door 't vol Leezen van goede Schrijvers" (A secretary becomes proficient by a close reading of good writers). Advertising himself as both *Geheymschryver der Stadt Amsterdam* and *Secretaris van Amsterdam*, Mostaert prefaces his volume with a tribute to the importance of letters heavily seasoned with self-consciously learned references to ancient as well as esteemed modern authors (Cicero, Seneca, Pliny, as well as Petrarch, Bembo, Erasmus, and Justus Lipsius) in a manner that was typical of the high classical prose style of the period. Like book jackets today, the preface also features promotions, including laudatory poems and prose endorsements by no less distinguished authors than the poet Hooft, the great scholar Caspar Barlaeus, and the burgomaster of Amsterdam. In the expanded and revised edition of 1656, the title page is decorated with an image of a professional letter writer—a *secretaris*, notary, or lawyer—seated at a writing desk with a quill pen handing a sealed letter to a client (*fig. 34*).

As with the earlier French manuals, Mostaert offers a range of model letters for various professional and personal situations, from letters of the law and introduction, business negotiations and solicitations, requests for mercy, reproaches, consolations, congratulations, even *Boertbrieven* (satirical letters). A whole section is devoted to the protocol of honorific modes of address, how one addresses the pope, a king, duke, burgomaster, ministers, and lesser mortals. It is hardly surprising that in 1595 the Archdukes Albert and Isabella of the Spanish Netherlands, where the ranks of minor nobles multiplied like Topsy, felt obliged to pass detailed laws specifying the titles and modes of address that various lords and dignitaries were permitted to use in public and on letters, but grandiose salutations also became fashionable in the more egalitarian society of Holland.[35] A professor at Leiden University might be greeted in a letter with a long and flattering Latin salutation, and it was only fitting when one wrote to the poet Hooft, who was properly Drost van Muiden (sheriff of Muiden), to address him as *edel, ernfeste, wijsheer* (noble, honorable, wise gentleman), but satires were written toward the end of the century ridiculing the inflation of honor, citing common young swells (*halfwassen brazempjes*) in coffeehouses who addressed each other as *mijnheer* and spoke of themselves in the third person.[36]

More rudimentary but almost as popular as Mostaert's manual was B. Hakvoord's *Algemeene zendbrieven* (Rotterdam, 1696), which was a primer for students. The preface emphasizes that this is a book designed to teach children, correct bad spelling, improve grammar, and a "kreupele Styl" (a lame writing style). It includes letters to meet basic daily needs—rent applications, contracts, testimonials, letters of collection, IOUs, wills, even prenuptial agreements, as well as thank-you letters, wedding announcements, and a selection of poetic greetings for New Year's, Easter, Pentecost, and the kermis. It is a measure of the targeted readership that the volume has a section devoted to riddles. Hakvoord, like Jacobi, maintains a high moral and religious tone in his letter models, but other later authors, like J. de Jongh Jr., who wrote *Post-comptoir van Cupido en Mercurius* (4th ed., 1766), admits in his introduction that some of his 320 letters are composed more for the reader's amusement than instruction.

Also often cited in lists of Dutch letter manuals is Pierre de la Chambre's *Verscheyden Brieven bequaem in de scholen ghebruycken* (Haarlem, 1648), written in French with Dutch translation, ostensibly by the master of a French school in Beverwyck. But the letters composing the brief exchange in this slim volume are intended less as models to follow than as a satire of the travails of a parent with a son away at school. It includes de la Chambre's letter of warning to the father, N. de la Montaigne, that his son is keeping "bad company and frequenting taverns and places of debauchery," the irate father's scolding letter to his son, his letter to the teacher assuring him of the reprimand, as well as a conciliatory second letter to the boy sent with the gift of a basket of pears. The fickle son's letters to the father range from requests to leave school and be delivered from his misery to permission to remain another semester. Predictably, it

concludes with schoolmaster's written request for payment of tuition fees. The spirit of this volume has less to do with exemplary letter manuals than with van de Passe's amusing print of *studentenleven* (*fig. 26*).

"Verscheyden minne-brieven—op allerey begevingen en gevallen" (Love Letters upon All Sorts of Subjects)

There are no love letters in Hakvoord's primer and only a tepid few in Mostaert's volume, but the last fifth of Puget de la Serre's *Le Secrétaire à la mode* is devoted to dozens of billets-doux under the heading given just above. The sample love letters he offers are not only responsive to one another but also to some degree progressive in their narrative of anonymous lovers' developing relationships. Most usefully, they offer multiple responses with varying degrees of ardor for the respondent to adjust the letter to be as reticent or encouraging, as restrained or insistent, as the individual situation required. Since the sample letters were read so extensively by Dutch audiences during the period in which the paintings in question were created, it is instructive to quote them at length in an attempt to evoke some of the associations contemporary viewers might have had when viewing images of young men and women with letters.

At the outset, the suitor might send the letter that appears under the anodyne title, "A Presentation of Service": "I should not take the Liberty to let you know how extreamly I honour you, if the Absolute power of your Beauty did not force me to it." Or he may write: "I must of necessity for my own Quiet declare the desire which I have, to love, and to serve you, if you Judge mee worthy of so great an honour." The lady who is the recipient of this gallant, impassioned missive is offered several options in replying. She can be politely demure: "I am much obliged to you for the good will you witnesse in my behalfe, but I have no other Liberty left mee, except to give you thanks as I do very humbly: assuring you that I will conserve your Remembrance for an acknowledgement." Or she could be more encouraging: ". . . though they be ordinary effects of your Civility, rather than Proofes of your love, yet I cannot chuse but be extreamly obliged to you, which I beseech you believe." Still another option was to avoid the issue by referring the suitor to her parents: ". . . my Will does so absolutely depend of my Parents inclination, that you are to learne of them, that which you desire to know of mee."

A final solution was not to answer the letter at all, but the implication is that this will only redouble the suitor's efforts, since the manual includes a whole series of letters begging or demanding a reply: "If you knew with what impatience I expect the favour of your Reply, I assure my selfe your Charity would oblige you to set my Mind at Quiet." When the lady finally writes back, she once again has the option to defer to her parents, though being subtly encouraging: "I took the Liberty to write unto you but not to resolve you in your request; You know the Quality of Daughter does so subject mee, that I cannot violate the Respect I save unto my Parents; yet I confesse myself much indebted to your good Nature." Or she can relent and write more openly: "I was resolved to keep silence, not knowing what answer to give you; but since you require a letter, this shall I tell you, that I have no other Resolution than to honour you as your Merit does oblige me: And that in requitall of your Civility, I shall make myselfe accounted in all places."

A constant theme of love letters in manuals is the letter of longing written to an absent lover. In Puget de la Serre's volume, such letters are dire and mount in their melodrama: "I suffer a Torment whose report only would force my Enemies to compassion, and yet can hardly believe that you regard it, being farre from imagining you are touched by it, in the least respect." And more extravagantly: "I passe over whole daies without eating, and whole Nights without sleep. . . . Judge now if I be not one of the most wretched Lovers in the World. Yet my Consolation is this, that I suffer all these Afflictions for the most worthy subject living, and for whom I would lose a Thousand Lives." The lady's optional responses include some wit and cold water: "Loves diseases are so easie to cure, that I never spend my Charity on such persons. If you be surprized with that kind of Malady, my Absence (whereof you complain) will soone afford you a Remedy; but if that should not prove as I expect, then (to your owne advantage) the truth of your Affection will appear by the continuance of your Constancy. . . ." Or another: "You know I am not accustomed to credit the Complaints of Lovers, because they dye so often in word and Appearance, that the report of their Afflictions does now passe for a Fable." Or still more harshly: "Cease then your discourse of Sorrows, and Griefs, and Sighes and Lamentations; 'tis a language that Molests me extreamly."

But under a heading titled "Other more obliging Answers," we read: "I am sensible of the Affliction which my absence causeth in you . . . you must of necessity resolve to be patient, since it is the only Remedy of your Ill." And still more adamantly, rebelling and risking her parents' wrath: "If I had the power to comfort you with my Presence, you should soone see mee where my Letter is now. But being under the Subjection of a Father and Mother, who give me not so much as the Liberty to write to you, all I can do is to steale it, to comfort you with the Hopes of my Returne. Believe me, Sir. I wish for it with Passion."

A perhaps surprising group of letters follows under such headings as "Letters Protesting Lose and Fidelity" and "Letters Complaining of Inconstancy." The latter ironically only include letters written by men to women, expressing bitterness but allowing that his love persists: "I never thought that after so many protestations of Fidelity, you would have lost even the remembrance of having made them. . . . live contented in your new Conquest . . . you will never find any that will equall my Affection." And another, more blunt and cutting: Your inconstancy has provoked in mee more Pitty, than it has procured me ill . . . because I have some respect to your Honour." The lady's responses are not contrite but combative: "I will give you an account of this Action when you please, and when you are truly informed how things passed, you will have no other Judge but yourself. . . ." And again the response of the daughter of overbearing parents: "If you knew with what violence I was constrain'd to this Mutation, I make no doubt that you would esteeme me far more worthy Praise, than Reproach. Imagine the power of a Tyrannicall Father towards his daughter under his obedience . . . I leave to your selfe to consider what I am able to doe against so strong an enemy." It is easy to see how the epistolary novel was soon to evolve. The volume concludes with two sample letters requesting keepsakes of one's sweetheart, namely a portrait likeness, "knowing I value the original more than all other things in the World" (see cat. 13), and a lock or "Bracelet of your Haire."

Puget de la Serre's tidy little volume is consistent with most love letter manuals of the period, which begin with a highly formal declaration of affection answered by a modest refusal, which provokes the suitor's escalating, hyperbolic expressions of ardor, culminating in a ritualistic threat of suicide, which may be assuaged and even tenderly rewarded by the lady after a respectable delay. But at this point there usually follow different options and voices for the woman: she may remain chaste despite the supplications of her lover; express her hindrance in the promise of marriage by the will of her father; or, in the case of a married woman, express her qualms and temptations at the prospect of adultery, which then often devolves into mutual accusations of infidelity. All of these personae subsequently enter into exchanges that alternate in varying degrees between passion and high anxiety.

The Sources and Course of Love Letters

In his brief but invaluable survey of French letter manuals from 1550 to 1700, Bernard Bray cited among the most important sources for exemplary love letters, Ovid's *Heroides* and the famous medieval love letters of Héloïse and Abélard.[37] The latter were the learned and impassioned correspondence between the twelfth-century scholastic philosopher and logician, who helped found the University of Paris, and his talented pupil and young lover, Héloïse. Her uncle was a powerful canon who when he discovered that Abélard had seduced and married his niece had him castrated. Abélard became a monk in the abbey of St.-Denis and continued to teach theology but ran afoul of the official church. Héloïse became the abbess of the convent of the Paraclete that Abélard had founded. The correspondence between the two is one of the classic models of brilliantly eloquent letters, including the letter of consolation, the complimentary letter, and the tenderly sentimental love letter, but also conveys an uninhibited ecstatic passion. While Abelard, a changed man physically and spiritually, sees his condition as just punishment for his sins and tries to convert Héloïse to a similar chaste vision, she, unimpaired, writes fervently of her physicality: "The pleasures of lovers that we shared have scarcely been banished from my thoughts. Wherever I turn they are always there before my eyes, bringing with them awakened longings and fantasies which will not even let me sleep. Even during the celebration of Mass, when our prayers should be purer, lewd visions of those pleasures take such a hold on my unhappy soul that my thoughts are on their wantonness instead of on prayers."[38] Their letters appeared in François de Grenaille's *Nouveau recueil de lettres des dames tant anciennes que modernes* (1642), where they were described as *lettres chrétiennes* rather than *lettres d'amours*, and were anthologized several times during the seventeenth century.

Better known to Dutch audiences were the *Heroides* of Ovid (43 b.c.–a.d. 18) that were translated into French in 1598, 1605, and repeatedly thereafter, and into Dutch by the poet Jacob Westerbaen under the title *Eenige brieven van doorluchtige vrouwen* (1657; Some letters by illustrious women). Ovid's letters from the women of classical literature also were inserted into letter manuals, appearing at least as early as the second edition of the *Fleurs de bien dire* (1605). The *Heroides* are imaginary amatory letter poems that Ovid composed early in his career, ostensibly written by the great heroines of mythology and legend (borrowed primarily from Homer and Virgil) to lovers and husbands far away. Though sometimes judged by Ovid's brilliantly vivid later standards as overly rhetorical, the letters offered models of the remarkably strong and candid voices of women in the straits of love, be they pining, abandoned, infatuated, abashed, or aroused. Here we meet the faithful Penelope who writes to her husband, Ulysses, "Yours I am, and yours I must be called"; the vain and fickle Helen, who claims that Paris's confession of his love has "profaned my eyes" but adds coyly, "your beauty, too, I confess is rare,"

and, acquiescing to a delayed meeting, allows fatefully that it "may be friendly to your wish"; or the wonderfully irrepressible young love of Hero for her strong swimming Leander: "I cannot be patient for Love! We burn with equal fires, but I am not equal to you in strength; men methinks must have stronger natures. As the body, so is the soul of women frail. Delay but a little longer and I shall die!"[39] The ready access of these classical literary models no doubt emboldened women to return the favor of a frank and candid letter from an admirer.

There is also some evidence to suggest that personal letters became more open and direct over the course of the seventeenth century. In a piece entitled "Du style épistolaire" published in July 1683 in a special edition of *Mercure gallant*, Le Fevrerie ridiculed the "bizarre civility" of the highly artificial *lettre de compliment* and even claimed that letters "n'ont point de règles précises et certaines" (have no precise and certain rules), since they convey the uniqueness of the individual writer's personal situation.[40] The terms *sincère, franc*, and *simple* are now given more weight in discussions of the qualities essential to letter dialogues. Love letters are even celebrated as the truest form of authentic communication; in his *Traité sur la manière d'écrire des lettres et sur le ceremonial. . . .* (Paris, 1709), J. L. de Grimarest exempts the love letter from any rules of epistolary style, and in the third edition (1705) of Pierre Richelet's *Les plus belles lettres*, he introduces a new section entitled "Lettres passionnées," which du Plaisir even claims express the lover's thoughts more clearly than speech, "On ne garde point de règle dans les letters passionnées; la véhémence, l'inégalité, les doutes, les tumults, tout y a place; et de même qu'ailleurs on écrit comme on parle, ici on écrit comme l'on pense" (One honors no rules in letters of passion; the vehemence, the imbalance, the doubts, the tempestuousness, all have their place; and just as elsewhere one writes as one speaks, here one writes as one thinks).[41]

Dutch Literature and Letter Poems

An often-overlooked expression of the interest in letters in this period and their status as a uniquely familiar literary style is the *dichtbrief*, or letter poem. Letters were not only a popular pastime and means of communication but also an accepted art form in seventeenth-century Dutch literature, notwithstanding the dominance of a classical ideal and the didactic, often Christian and/or moral thrust of much of their poetry and prose.[42] Most seventeenth-century Dutch authors aspired to an international standard of classical literacy expressed in Latin, regarded as the ideal language of intellectual discourse. Though proud of their often-halting command of the lingua franca and rising in a few cases to become published poets, Dutch artists had no comparable international gold standard of painting.[43] A poet and painter might have the same vivid perceptions and expressive needs, but they were constrained by the respective conventions of their art forms. Consequently, seventeenth-century Dutch literature was much less naturalistic than the paintings for which Dutch culture is primarily remembered. Most Dutch poets, like their international brethren, aspired to the Aristotelian ideal of the expression of universal truths discovered in general observations. Whereas Dutch painting often celebrated the individual human detail, the goal of literature was to transcend the incidental and anecdotal. Dutch genre painting focused on the lives of everyday people, while Dutch literature rarely dwelt on the familiar or the domestic, even when featuring members of the upper classes. Much of Dutch theater, for example, is centered on the lives of royalty, which was distinctly unreal in the republic. One catches glimpses of the common man in the plays of Bredero who reportedly was a painter himself (though none of his paintings has been identified) and famously wrote in the introduction to his *Groot Lied-Boeck* (1622), "Het zijn de beste schilders, die 't leven naest komen" (The best painters are those who come closest to life). The poetics of the particular are also revealed in the writings of Jan Six van Chandelier. But most Dutch literature is written for learned humanistic circles with a penchant for the classics and aspirations to the universal statement.

The letter poem was popularized in the Renaissance but had its roots in antiquity. Cicero acknowledged the importance of personal as well as official letters to maintain contact and sustain friendships. Horace's epistolary poetry (*Epistulae*) proved to be the most enduring, being at once learned and conversational. Seneca affirmed the familiar style, suggesting that letters should be written as if you were strolling and conversing with the recipient. The *dichtbrief* is therefore exceptional in seventeenth-century Dutch literature in its promotion of a familiar, conversational voice and the discussion of personal details, even trivialities. The letter was defended as literature by the theorist G. J. Vossius (1630), who cited its classical precedents as an accepted literary type, albeit of lesser style. In her analysis of the *dichtbrief*, M. A. Schenkeveld-van der Dussen has observed that it was practiced with varying results, from the most pedestrian and mundane verse when written by the *predikant* J. Vollenhove (1686), or surprisingly disjointed poetry mixing high rhetoric and mundane confidences when attempted by the talented Bredero, but it occasionally attains a pleasing balance between the familiar and the literary, as for example in the poetry of D. V. Coornheert.[44] For an early-eighteenth-century poet like

H. K. Poot, who discussed the functions and attraction of letter poems in the second volume of his *Gedichten* (1728), it is their unconstrained, relaxed language that most appeals to him. But the epistolary poem was far less successful than the letter paintings produced in Holland that give pictorial form to this charming obsession.

As Schenkeveld-van der Dussen concludes, these poems point to later developments in modern literature that permitted more direct communication between the author and the reader. The pretext of the *dichtbrief* is a private letter written to a friend; but the poem itself is published, hence shared with the public, who becomes, as it were, a second reader who looks over the intended's shoulder. Thus the reader's role is that of a confidante, who is welcomed into the poet's circle of friends. This is a source of the powerful aura of confidentiality in both letter poems and those letter paintings by ter Borch, Metsu, and others (see *figs. 11, 12* and cat. 4) that depict a man or a woman peering over the back of the letter reader or writer. The effect of the eavesdropper is almost voyeuristic in its suggestiveness.

Ideals and Actualities: Petrarchism, Jacob Cats, and Real Letters

One of the ideals of seventeenth-century Dutch literature that probably influenced viewers' perceptions of love letter themes in paintings was the beautiful verse of the fourteenth-century Italian poet Petrarch. Part of the appeal of Petrarch's sublime poetry is the aching desire created by an insurmountable divide in gender relations. Petrarch posited a relationship between the sexes that invariably cast the man as the infatuated victim and martyr, and the woman as the coldhearted and aloof beauty, forever hovering tantalizingly beyond the suitor's grasp until he declines into melancholy and death. The poet-suitor adoringly inventories the lady's physical charms in versified catalogues, but his ardor is never requited. Petrarchan rhetoric became an ideal of amatory literature and love poetry throughout Renaissance and Baroque Europe, influencing, for example, the *Emblemata Amatoria* (1611) of Hooft, whose testament to his own personal suffering in love is preserved in an actual tear-stained love letter signed in his own blood (*fig. 35*).[45] The notion of the belle dame sans merci captured many a poetic imagination in this era. There is evidence, for example, that Petrarchism was a concept familiar to the family of the painter Gerard ter Borch.[46] The love poems that fill the album called "De papiere Lauwekrans" of Gerard's half-sister and favorite model, Gesina ter Borch, are peppered with Petrarchan diction and rhetoric. Gesina seems to have developed a relationship with an Amsterdam merchant and amateur poet, Hendrik Joris, but never married. Gerard ter Borch himself made a charming little drawing, *Young Man Kneeling before a Lady in a Love Garden* (fig. 36), which features a cupid to one side and a stag to the other—the elements of Daniel Heinsius's emblem of the doomed Pertrarchan lover, suggesting that he, too, had a developed understanding of the roles played by the genders in the ideal Petrarchan relationship.[47]

However, it would be a gross oversimplification to assume that the subtleties of ter Borch's ladies in satin are resolved by such a constricted literary formula. Women in his paintings enter into such surprisingly rich and often compromising situations with men, scarcely restricted to the psychologically suggestive exchanges or sidelong glances, but extending to obscene hand gestures, parried offers of venal love, and, eventually, to drinking some of their menfolk under the table (see cat. 10, *figs. 1 & 2*).[48] Ter Borch's women, like so many of the females in Dutch genre paintings, are far more interesting, full-blooded, and complex than the bewitching ice-goddesses of the Petrarchan ideal.

While Petrarch might be the literary staple of Hooft and the erudite Muiderkring (the poets and intellectuals who gathered at his country estate in Muiden), Jacob Cats was the unchallenged best-seller among the educated middle classes. He became the most popular living poet and moralist in the Netherlands in the seventeenth century. His *Houwelyck* (1625) is a monumental poetic tribute to exemplary female conduct progressively described through the successive stages of a woman's life. In the section called "Trouringh" there is a dialogue between a young unmarried woman, Rosette, and a slightly older, recently married woman, Sibille, about the dangers of composing love letters, which makes clear the censorious attitude that many took toward the fashion:

> *Rosette:*
> *Neem eens, ick kreegh een jonghman life,*
> *Sal ick niet soetjens, met een brief,*
> *Hem mogen klagen mijnen noot?*
> *'t Papier en kent geen eerbaer root,*
> *Den pen en inckt doen menighwerf*
> *Dat mont en tonge iet en derf.*

> *Sibille:*
> *Te schrijven aen een jongh gesel,*
> *En voeghde noyt een vrijster wel;*
> *Uw geode name, o sedigh dier,*
> *En moet niet hangen aen papier;*
> *Of iemant schoon een woort ontvalt,*
> *Wanneer de jeught te samen malt,*
> *Dat vlieght daer henen met den wint,*
> *Soo dat'er niemant weder vint;*
> *Maer niet dat soo geduerigh blijft,*
> *Als dat een stoute penne schrijft;*

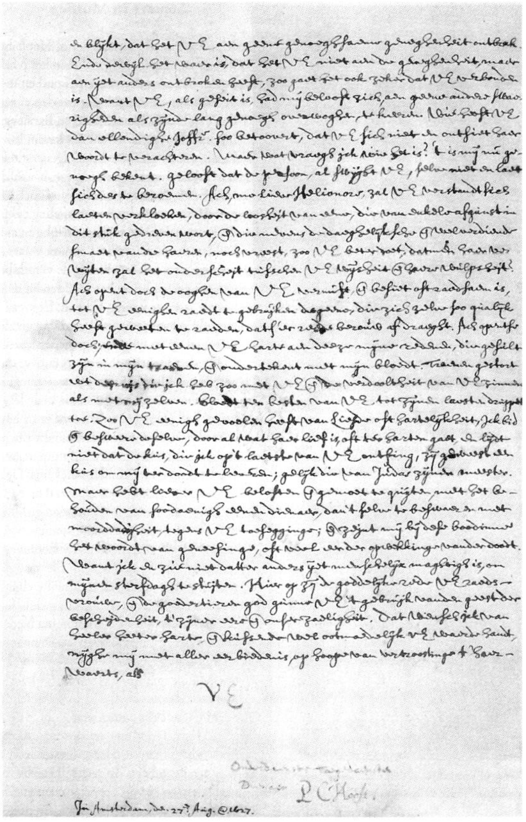

Fig. 35. The last page of P. C. Hooft's letter to Leonora Hellemans, dated August 27, 1627
Universiteitsbibliotheek, Leiden, sign. Pap. 13H1

Fig. 36. Gerard ter Borch
Young Man Kneeling before a Lady in a Love Garden
Pencil on paper, 15.3 x 19.9 cm
Rijksprentenkabinet, Amsterdam, no. A812

En koomt'er dan eenquade slagh,
Als dickmael tusschen liefjens plagh,
Soo wort uw brief, tot smaet en jock,
Gehangen aen de groote klock,
Oock is'er geen ontkennen aen,
Men siet de ronde letters staen:
En schoon het u ten hooghsten spijt,
Ghy moet dan lijden het verwijt;
Dus, hebje schaemt' en eere life,
En schrijft noyt dwasen minne-brief.

(Rosette:
For example, if I am fond of a young man,
Should I not take the time to express my feelings in a letter,
That he might know my longing?
Paper doesn't know how to blush.
Pen and ink can often speak in a way
That the mouth and tongue would not allow.

Sibille:
To write to a young fellow
Is never becoming for a maid;
Your good name, oh demure creature,
Must not be committed to paper;
If someone even lets one word slip out
When the youth gather,
It flies hither with the wind,
So that no one can find it again;
Yet it is not as enduring
As that which is written by the bold pen;
And there follows a quarrel,
As often arises between lovers,
So your letter, and its outrageous statements,
Is announced to the public
And there is no denying it,
The big letters are clearly visible,
And leaves you with the greatest regret,
You will then suffer reproaches;
Thus have you shamed honorable love;
Never write stupid love letters.)[49]

If "Vader" Cats was not the best of Holland's poets, he nonetheless became her official conscience, forever hectoring young women about proper behavior and successfully capturing the middle-brow imagination. Yet while Cats's *Houwelyck* might seem little more than a conduct manual, love letters were taken very seriously in this period; indeed, they were admissible evidence in breach-of-promise suits brought before church councils; and they might be submitted as proof of a suitor's intentions in lieu of a marriage contract or engagement ring.[50] Moralists like Adriaen Poirters fulminated against the language used in love letters: "There is nothing more common today than the words used in love letters: 'My Goddess, my heart, my soul, I will be your slave as long as I live, until death gathers me, until the grave.'"[51] And the emblematist Johan de Brune complained of the cloyingly adoring nicknames used as forms of address in

love letters: "To Her Royal Highness, the Queen of my Heart."[52] But the public seemed to enjoy this hyperbolic language; in the playwright van Santen's *Snappende Sytgen* (1624), May describes a love letter in which "He called me his joy, his consolation, his beloved love, his lodestar, his goddess, and a thousand similar things."[53] And the revelation of the contents of love letters was a common premise of farces of the period.[54]

While the pictorial and theatrical conventions might suggest that the majority of private letters were written by suitors and lovers, a recent sampling of actual letters written by women in this period reminds us that letters had a wide range of purposes and functions, though most were designed to strengthen a network of friendships and social relations.[55] Since the majority of these letters have been gleaned from published sources, often anthologies of famous men's letters, they are mostly written to men by women, most of whom were members of the *gegoede burgerij*, or well-to-do citizenry. Yet these letters manage to evoke a richly nuanced if small social circle, particularly that of the family of Constantijn Huygens in The Hague. Huygens's proper and rather severe mother, Susanna Hoefnagel, writes to her youthful son in the early 1620s, when he was stationed in London on a diplomatic mission reporting on everything from politics to the rain-drenched letter courier who arrives just at dinnertime to dispense letters around the table, family news, recent parties and marriages, his sister's sore throat, and, in closing, submits a request for corks for her beer jugs (even the upper classes were hard-pressed to find potable drinking water). Huygens's eldest sister, Geertruijt, writes in the same period, launching straight into her account with scarcely a salutation and no regard for rules of composition, describing the exertions and cost in domestic renovations that the family had recently endured in trying to lure the famously beautiful Suzanne van Baerle to marry Huygens's older brother, Maurits. It is a measure of the small radius of this circle of friends that Suzanne was later wooed by the widower Hooft, who was eighteen years her senior, and eventually wed Constantijn Huygens himself (*see figs. 1, 37*). However, in this particular campaign, Geertruijt scolds Maurits for having no interest in singing and playing music, for having made little or no effort in the courtship, and who, she contemptuously concludes, is a *saaie boel* (a dull sort). Constantijn's other sister, Constance, pens a breezy letter, apologizing for her haste and poor penmanship, but pleading with him to bring her back from London a *zwart pluimpje* (black feather), then all the rage.

Perhaps the most spontaneous and informal of these letters comes from the Huygens's effervescent next-door neighbor Dorothea van Dorp. Three years Constantijn's senior, she initiated him romantically when he was a youth (Constantijn wrote her fifteen letters in French and even composed poems and an anagram on her name[56]) and still refers to him by her pet name, "Song" (see epigraphs, above). While his letters to her do not survive, she confesses she is flattered that he writes to her at such length about political matters and begs for more long letters, but disapproves of his practice (presumably admitted openly in his own lost correspondence) of visiting prostitutes and also seems ambivalent about his relationship with Lady Killegrew (she concludes one such letter: "Goodbye Song, I'm in a bad mood [ik ben in een malle steming]"). Yet her letters convey a generosity, vitality, and spontaneity that are without literary pretension and have a remarkably modern tone.

Other letters from this period, by contrast, for example Maria Tesselschade Roemer Visscher's letters to Hooft, assume an artificial literary manner contrived to appeal to her learned friend and mentor. Even more stilted in their wordplay and self-consciously literate style are the letters of an ambitious poetess, Alida Bruno, to Huygens. Naturally not all letters deal with love or literature; the letters to the great jurist and theologian Hugo de Groot from his brave wife, Maria van Reigersberch, who famously orchestrated his escape from prison in a chest, speak not of courage but of enduring bitterness and perennial anxiety. And the daughter Suzanna of the renowned scholar Caspar Barlaeus, who chose not to follow her father's intellectual lead or strive for the literary aspirations of the Visscher sisters but became instead a deeply pious and religious woman, writes scrupulously formal, reserved letters to her future watchmaker-poet husband, only agreeing to marry him after a protracted courtship during which she gradually progresses from addressing him as *waarde vriend* (worthy friend) to *aller liefste* (most charming), but still will not agree to marry him (despite the arrival of their first child) until he has dutifully trained for the clergy and become a minister.

Emblematics and the Vanity of Letters

Emblem books also reveal seventeenth-century associations about letters and the power of written documents. For Roemer Visscher, who composed the popular emblem book *Sinnepoppen* (Amsterdam, 1614), documents and letters were not worth the paper they were written on without a proper seal of authentication (*fig. 38*).[57] A Visscher emblem depicting a disembodied hand composing at a writing desk warns of the dangers of secretaries, notaries, and others entrusted with important documents and letters straying from the truth (*fig. 39*).[58] The emblem book by Otto Vaenius, who was Peter Paul Rubens's teacher, entitled *Amorum Emblemata* (Antwerp, 1608), reflected the new fashion for love

Fig, 37. Jacob van Campen
Double Portrait of Constantijn Huygens and Susanna van Baerle, c. 1635
Oil on canvas, 95 x 78.5 cm
Royal Cabinet of Paintings, Mauritshuis, The Hague, no. 1089

Dat cera fidem.

Periculum in declinatione.

Fig. 38. Emblem entitled *Dat cera fidem* from Roemer Visscher's
Sinnepoppen (1614), no. XLVI
Library, Faculty of Arts, Utrecht University

Fig. 39. Emblem entitled *Periculum in declinatione* from Roemer
Visscher's *Sinnepoppen* (1614), no. LVI
Library, Faculty of Arts, Utrecht University

Fig. 40. Cupid and a Messenger
Emblem from Otto Vaenius, *Amorum emblemata. . . .* (Antwerp,
1608), p. 132
Library, Faculty of Arts, Utrecht University

Fig. 41. Cupid Presenting a Letter to a Maiden
Emblem from Jan Harmensz. Krul, *Pampiere Wereld*
(Amsterdam, 1644), vol. 2
Koninklijke Bibliotheek, The Hague (2148 E4 p. 81 dl. 3)

letters, depicting a cupid seated reading a letter on a
hillock in the company of a letter messenger with his
traditional staff, cape, and hat *(fig. 40).*[59] Quoting Seneca,
Vaenius observes that letters are traces of love. In the
illustrations of Jan Harmensz. Krul's *Pampiere Wereld*
(Amsterdam, 1644), Cupid himself delivers letters, in
one case to a well-dressed young woman seated in a
comfortable interior much like those that we encounter
in Dutch genre paintings *(fig. 41);* according to Krul,
she personifies "vrijsters die minnen, en hebben geen
zinnen" (maids who fall in love but have no sense).[60]
Another illustration from Krul's play *Rozemond*
again shows Cupid in the role of *Liefds bode* (Love's
messenger), offering to take a letter from the lovesick
heroine to the object of her affection (see cat. 15, *fig. 1*),
which prompts her to philosophize on the quandaries
of love, letters, and the suspicions they arouse.[61] Letters
also figure prominently in Jan Steen's comically theatrical
paintings of the doctor's visit (see cat. 32), in which the
diagnosis of the lady's illness is invariably lovesickness
or pregnancy.

Letter writing, especially love letters, was also
sometimes regarded as a vain pastime and figured in
symbolic images admonishing the viewer about the
fleeting, transitory nature of worldly existence. One
particularly highly charged image is Hendrick Pot's
Allegory of Vanity from the 1630s in the Frans
Halsmuseum *(fig. 42).*[62] It depicts an interior with an
elegantly dressed lady seated in the center, smiling and
looking out directly at the viewer, with one hand on her
hip and the other holding a letter. She is surrounded by
precious jewels, musical instruments (the tones of which
are fleeting), and, on the floor to left, a mirror (a time-
honored *vanitas* symbol) beside a cat (a notoriously
sensuous and unreliable beast) wearing a preposterously
vain pearl necklace. If the thrust of these details were
ot clear enough, an old woman, presumably a serving
woman, leans over the woman's shoulder holding a rose

in one hand (the flower that will soon fade) and the ultimate *vanitas* symbol, a death's-head. In another painting by Pot in the Museum of Fine Arts, Boston, a woman sits amid piles of similarly transitory treasures but strikes a more somber expression, probably because as in other *vanitas* images of ladies in their boudoirs (see, for example, Hendrick Hondius's *Vanitas* engraving after a design by Jacob de Gheyn) she seems to have originally been embraced by a skeleton, later painted out by a squeamish owner.[63] As Otto Naumann has observed, it seems probable that Frans van Mieris's several paintings of an elegant lady admiring herself in a mirror before tables on which an open letter appears with a broken seal also resonate with vanitas associations (*fig. 43*).[64]

Letters in Misunderstood and "Modern" Histories

Some letter themes in Dutch art appear outwardly to modern audiences as genre scenes but in fact are history paintings. For example, the painting by Nicholas Knüpfer of the swooning young lady in a yellow and blue gown with her foot on a foot warmer and holding a letter (cat. 27) at first glance might seem to depict simply another dramatic young lady succumbing to bad news and the vapors. However, her costume is not seventeenth-century attire; indeed, it is sufficiently exotic to alert us to a subject from history or literature. In the presence of the expiring heroine, the covered cup probably contains poison, and the alarmed serving woman at the back helps confirm the identification of the protagonist as the Carthaginian seductress, Sophonisba, whose fateful story was told by Livy and Cats and was treated in several paintings by Knüpfer. We include this history painting in the exhibition not merely to remind the viewer of our susceptibility to misinterpreting subjects as anonymous genre but also because its theme and treatment recall a passage from the classical art theorist Gerard de Lairesse, who was scathing in his criticism of history paintings that treated subjects in a "modern" manner without sufficient attention to the historical accuracy of details:

> One can find painters whose boldness is laughable, and who dare to represent a Sophonisba dressed entirely in today's fashion, with a velvet jacket, a white satin skirt with gold trim, lace sleeves, fake curls on her head, white slippers on her feet, and that in a room hung with gold leather . . . and furnished with velour chairs. . . . the chimneypiece with large china dishes. . . . One sees a Moor approaching, who offers her a contemporary gold goblet or crystal glass, on a silver platter being dressed in livery with cords and tassels. Her fancy bed has not been forgotten down to the pewter or silver pisspot. . . .[65]

Fig. 42. Hendrick Pot
Allegory of Vanity, c. 1633
Oil on panel, 61 x 83 cm
Frans Halsmuseum, Haarlem, no. 469a

Fig. 43. Frans van Mieris
Woman Admiring Herself in a Mirror, c. 1662
Oil on panel, 30 x 23 cm
Staatliche Museen zu Berlin, Preußischer Kulturbesitz
Gemäldegalerie, no. 838

While Knüpfer's history painting scarcely includes the many anachronisms that Lairesse so disdained in his imagined *Sophonisba*, the history paintings of Jan Steen frequently employ the outward appearance and accessories of genre painting. Perhaps his most extreme example of a history painting in the guise of genre is his *Bathsheba Receiving King David's Letter* (cat. 31), which could easily be mistaken for an exercise in high-life genre painting, with its seventeenth-century interior setting and woman's costume in the fashion of ter Borch's scenes of stylish, satin-clad ladies. Indeed, when Steen's painting was exhibited at the Royal Academy in London in 1878, it was entitled *Le Billet Doux*. However, the history subject is revealed by the inscription on the letter that she holds: *alder / Schonte / Bersabe / omdat*. As Mariët Westermann has observed, this is precisely the type of picture that provoked Lairesse's screed.[66] It is a remarkable treatment of one of the most popular biblical subjects in Dutch art and the theme most readily associated with a letter. In a lecture in praise of painting delivered in 1642, Philips Angel commended Jan Lievens for having considered the Bathsheba story thoroughly enough to realize that David must have propositioned Bathsheba not simply with a messenger bringing a verbal message but with a letter, "as evidence of a greater authority," even though no such letter is mentioned in the Bible; and, further, that it was likely carried by a "an

old woman well versed in the art of love, or a procuress."[67] The bent and wizened old woman in the Steen conforms to the procuress type. Steen's comical painting in Budapest of a prostitute in a brothel holding a letter (cat. 33) has also sometimes been interpreted as a Bathsheba subject. There, too, the procuress appears at the back receiving payment from a client. When Rembrandt addressed the subject in his great and magisterial painting of 1654 in the Louvre (*fig. 44*), he treated it as a history painting, even depicting Bathsheba in the nude, recalling the biblical reference to David first spying her as she bathed (II Sam. 11:2). But Rembrandt also includes an old serving woman who resembles the procuress type and gives Bathsheba a letter. His genius parts company with the other painters in giving Bathsheba a meditative expression, which mixes a smile with a hint of melancholy, the perfect combination of physical temptation and remorse, since after Bathsheba slept with David, the king sent her husband into battle to be killed. Steen's version of *Bathseba after the Bath* in the J. Paul Getty Museum, Los Angeles (cat. 31, *fig. 2*), seems to be in part inspired by the Rembrandt, but in that work, *Bathsheba Receiving David's Letter* (cat. 31), and most clearly in his *Bathsheba with the Letter* (inscribed "Schoon[ste] Bersa[bé]") in a private collection (*fig. 45*), Bathsheba looks out unabashedly at the viewer, even smiling openly in the last work mentioned.

Fig. 44. Rembrandt van Rijn
Bathsheba after the Bath, 1654
Oil on canvas, 142 x 142 cm
Musée du Louvre, Paris, inv. M.I. 957

Fig. 45. Jan Steen
Bathesheba with the Letter
Oil on canvas, 63 x 52 cm
Private Collection

Thus in Steen's various interpretations of the story the moral choice and quandary posed by David's letter seem to be resolved. In figure 45, Bathsheba may strike the pose, with head in hand, traditionally associated with Melancholia, but she smiles with lustful and contented resignation to her fate. In his lovely little picture of 1671 in Dresden (cat. 25), van Mieris does not show us Bathsheba's expression, depicting her in profile, although her relaxed body language as she sits again with head in hand but dangling her arm over the chair back, casually holding the letter, suggests that she will be receptive to the offer, described with such enumerating salesmanship and importunate gusto by the ugly procuress on the far side of the table. And in van Mieris's recently discovered painting of 1680 (cat.26), the procuress type and the opened letter again beg the question of whether the smiling woman is a vain and willing, modern Bathsheba. However, sometimes in Dutch genre scenes women refuse to accept a letter and its potential for moral dilemma. In ter Borch's *The Rejected Letter* in the Alte Pinakothek, Munich, for example (cat. 8, *fig. 2*), a trumpeter enters with a letter, but the woman folds her arms, resolutely refusing to receive it and offers only a slight, wry smile and raised eyebrows. In the background beyond the messenger is a tapestry depicting a king with two other figures, suggesting to some that the activity in the foreground may recall Bathsheba's receipt of the propositioning letter.[68] Furthermore, the serving woman standing behind and to the right with a basin and ewer not only suggests that the messenger has disrupted the lady's toilette but may also symbolically allude to the purity that the woman's decisive refusal upholds (on this symbolism, see cat. 41). The capacity of letters for bringing portentous news and moral crises is obviously a factor in the startled or unsettled expressions that greet their arrival in works, for example, by Vermeer (see Vergara essay, *figs. 57 & 58*).

Paintings-within-Paintings and Other Signifiers

A time-honored device used by genre artists to comment on their subjects was the painting-within-the-painting, which in conjunction with a letter can imply something about the latter's unseen contents. In the background of Dirck Hals's painting of a contented-looking woman with a letter, for example, there is a calm seascape (cat. 2), while in the background of his image of a woman tearing up a letter (*fig. 2*) there is a rough marine, suggesting that the absent writer may have met with ill fortune.[69] Seascapes also appear at the back of Metsu's *Woman Reading a Letter with a Maidservant* (cat. 19) and Vermeer's *Love Letter* (*fig. 58*), suggesting that these ladies, too, receive their letters from a seafaring traveler. Seventeenth-century literature often likened the

course of love to a sea journey; Jan Harmensz. Krul wrote in 1640, "Love may rightly be compared with the sea / from the viewpoint of her changes / which one hour cause hope / the next fear: So too goes it with a lover / who like the skipper / who journeys to sea / one day encounters good weather / the next storms and roaring wind. . . ."[70] Sometimes the reference is more specific. In the background of Johannes Verkolje's painting of an officer with a lady friend receiving a letter from a military courier (cat. 42) there is a mural of the Death of Adonis, the hunter who against Venus's entreaties went hunting and was gored to death, a subject that was interpreted in the seventeenth century as an admonition against impetuous youth who disregard wise counsel. On the back wall of the *voorhuis* in Ludolph de Jongh's *Lady Receiving a Letter* (*fig. 20*) there is a large painting of Diana and Acteon (derived from a composition by Antonio Tempesta), showing the hunter who spied on the chaste goddess as she and her nymphs bathed and paid for his voyeurism with his life. The detail has been interpreted variously, as a witty commentary on the arrival of the letter as a form of male intrusion into a female world or, if one assumes the letter is a love letter, as a warning to its amorous author of the potential consequences of his actions.[71] There is little ambiguity about the meaning of the painting-within-the-painting in Steen's scene of a prostitute with a letter (cat. 33); it depicts the Prodigal Son driven from the whorehouse. Sometimes the signifier is not a painting but a sculpture. In the night scene by Nicholas Verkolje of a young lady waving a letter from a window (cat. 44) presumably to a suitor below, there is a facade stone (*gevelsteen*) with a relief of one of the laborers in the vineyards of Canaan with a huge bunch of grapes and the partially visible inscription "'t lant van de[lofte]" (The Promised Land). It is possible that the promise is the young lady herself, but it is more likely that this detail stands in moral opposition to her encouraging gestures; the grapes of Canaan were a traditional Eucharist symbol, referring to Christ's sacrifice that makes possible access to the promised land of heaven. Thus the detail, like others in the painter's work, probably functions as a moral admonition against the temptation of love letters and nocturnal trysts.

Epilogue: The Eighteenth Century and the Dutch Legacy

In 1669, when ter Borch, Metsu, de Hooch, and Vermeer had only recently executed some of their finest letter paintings, Madame de Sévigné (1626–1696) married her daughter to the comte de Grignan, who lived in Provence, and began one of the greatest long-distance literary correspondences in modern history, first

Fig. 46. Jean-Baptiste Siméon Chardin
Woman Sealing a Letter
Oil on canvas
Stiftung Preussische Schlösser und Gärten, Schloss
Charlottenburg, Berlin, no. GKI 4507

Fig. 47. Francisco José de Goya y Lucientes
The Letter, c. 1813–20
Oil on canvas, 181 x 125 cm
Musée des Beaux-Arts, Lille, no. P.9

Fig. 48. James Tissot
The Letter, c. 1876–78
Oil on canvas, 71.4 x 107.1 cm
National Gallery of Canada, Ottawa, purchased 1964,
no. 15191

published (posthumously) in a slim volume as *Lettres choisies de Madame la Marquise de Sévigné à Madame de Grignan sa fille* (1725) and greatly expanded with many more informal letters in editions of 1734–37; these amount to about 1,500 letters and attest to a mother's abiding affection for her daughter, but they also convey much more. Madame de Sévigné wrote letters on personal, literary, and social news, which chronicle her time and reveal her to be a woman of extraordinarily unaffected elegance and remarkable wit and intelligence. Particularly within the narrow confines of late-seventeenth-century French literature and society, her letters convey a freedom of personal autobiographical expression and feeling that are unprecedented in their casual frankness, even negligence, that find spiritual if not actual precedents in the naturalism of Dutch high-life domestic letter paintings.

The eighteenth century would bring epistolary literature to its height in both France and England, with writings of all kinds—topical, fictional, official, and private—all taking the forms of letters. In France one saw the publication of François Fénélon's *Lettres à l'Académie* (1714), Charles-Louis Montesquieu's *Lettres persanes* (1721), François Voltaire's *Lettres anglaises* (1734), Honoré Mirabeau's *Lettres à Sophie* (1792), and Charles de Brosses's *Lettres familières*. Denis Diderot and his friend Jean-Jacques Rousseau wrote famously eloquent letters,

as did so many others (the prince de Ligne, Mademoiselle de Lespinasse, and Madame du Deffard, who corresponded with Horace Walpole), and, as in England but more rarely in Holland, epistolary novels appeared, Rousseau's *Julie, ou La Nouvelle Héloïse* (1761) and Pierre Choderlos de Laclos's *Les Liaisons dangereuses* (1782). Private love letters multiplied, taking every form and tone from innocent flirtations to outrageous libertinage, and often were purloined and published. Furniture (*secrétaires, bureaux, escritoires, chiffoniers*, and the ladies' writing desk called the *bonheur-du-jour*) as well as the other decorative arts were confected and conscripted into service to the new rage for letters. In paintings, the letter continued to be a central theme in important works by artists like Jean-Siméon Chardin (*fig. 46*), François Boucher (Timken Museum of Art, San Diego), Jean-Honoré Fragonard (The Metropolitan Museum of Art, New York), and Francisco Goya (*fig. 47*). J.-B. Santerre carried on the tradition of the letter theme in pendants, but in the hands of artists like Alexis Grimou and Jean Roaux (Musée du Louvre, Paris), the theme became increasingly anecdotal and slight. While there continued to be profound letter paintings executed in the nineteenth century (Jacques-Louis David's *Death of Marat*, Edouard Manet's *Emile Zola*—although both are portraits—and genre scenes by Jean-Baptiste-Camille Corot, Ernest Meissonier, Mary Cassatt, Berthe Morisot,

act of writing had previously been confined to men, save for a few aristocratic women.[17] Vermeer's dedication to exploring femininity in his art was so sustained, however, that this adaptation of a largely masculine prototype to a contemporary Dutchwoman should not be surprising. Furthermore, the ways in which he accentuated the letter writer's gaze, and integrated it within the painting, typify his artistic intelligence. He rendered each of her eyes as a distinct point of light on velvety brown, and made that design echo throughout the scene. On a slightly larger scale, numerous such points of light glow against dark—three dense constellations decorating the box; one on her earring at right; two lines of them forming metal studs on her chair; and a single one on the chair behind the table.[18]

This lady might well be construed as writing a love letter. In the large painting-within-the-painting, much obscured with time, a bass viol remains visible, hinting at the association between music and love that occurs so frequently in Vermeer's oeuvre. And the empty chair might again stand surrogate for an absent person, to whom she writes the letter. But the background picture, even originally, was probably not clear enough to provide a strong interpretative clue, and the further chair is muted. In this case, perhaps equally important as the love theme, is letter writing in general as proper to higher-class, educated Dutchwomen. A recently published collection from the pens of eleven of them makes this quite clear.[19]

Now to consider Vermeer's three epistolary scenes wherein both a mistress and a maid play starring roles (fig. 51). The painter markedly describes differences in social condition between the two women, while at the same time contriving for neither to emerge unequivocally "on top." Symptomatically, a document of 1675 describes the mistress and maid in one of these scenes as simply "two personages" (see cat. 39). Vermeer's novel undercutting of some standard social hierarchies is bound up with the situation in which a maid transmits private letters for a lady, creating special intimacy between the two women. The idea depends partly on such literary sources as Ovid's *Art of Love* and its many chaste adaptations in Dutch.[20]

Probably the first in Vermeer's series, *Mistress and Maid* (fig. 57), like all his works, plays on theme and variations. Here, for example, he incorporated the dark background and many motifs from *A Lady Writing* (fig. 55). But only *Mistress and Maid* combines an impressively immediate close-up view with life-size figures. The basic narrative is simple, its implications complex. The lady had been writing a letter, but now the servant brings her to a halt by arriving with one from outside. Vermeer presents this interruption as momentous

Fig. 57. Johannes Vermeer
Mistress and Maid, c. 1667–1669
Oil on canvas, 90.2 x 78.7 cm
The Frick Collection, New York, acc. no. 19.1.126

for the mistress. He indicates her concerned response through gestures that we perceive as having occurred nearly simultaneously, and involuntarily, which makes them all the more convincing. She has pushed away from the table; set down her pen; uttered a surprised reaction—her jaw drops (daintily, to be sure); and entered into a state of quick mental deliberation. Still holding the lowered quill in her right hand, she presses her left fingertips to her chin, a stability-creating move necessary for absorbing the fact and significance of the incoming letter. The rendering of the eye visible in the mistress's profile view constitutes a technically radical touch—indeed, a faint smudge. This, too, has an expressive goal. It is as if her eyes have gone suddenly blank as she searches her mind; she looks neither at the letter nor the maid. The neon-bright, zigzagging ornament around her chignon suggests nothing so much as racing thoughts. Further, the agitated folds in the table covering and her jacket—so different from the calm effect in *A Lady Writing*—externalize the tumult of her inner emotion.[21]

Arthur Wheelock writes of this painting: "The mistress' expression reveals the uncertainties of love that disrupt the serenity of ordered existence. The mistress' controlled demeanor and fashionable wardrobe seem to suggest that such fleeting doubts affect even those who are most secure and content in their lives."[22] "Secure and content" in this context denotes prosperity, education, youth, and attractiveness. Through the maid, Vermeer dramatizes this privileged state in a series of categorical contrasts: the lady's elegance versus the servant's plainness; the seated woman's stable, expansive form versus the maid's slightly awkward carriage; the mistress's extreme blond tonality versus her subordinate's shadowed skin and deeper-colored clothing. In light of all these differences, only slowly does the realization dawn that the maid appears to be the same age as the mistress, with a face just as good; so too all the rest, as far as we can see. As in all three mistress-and-maid paintings, Vermeer makes us freshly aware of heightened femininity as a socioeconomic construct. In this example, the maid, by comparison, even seems a bit masculine: her hair much obscured by the surrounding darkness, and her clothed shape less rounded than the mistress's, whose fullness Vermeer accentuates with two orange ribbons curving over her lap.

The artist sets up yet other polarities between maid and mistress—frontal versus profile; left versus right; ongoing versus arrested motion. Not inherently hierarchical, these distinctions nevertheless create pictorial equilibrium—and with it a certain version of equality that Vermeer clearly sought. Always, he placed the servant higher in the pictorial field. In this painting, the maid's lowered gaze, traversing the dark gap at center,

settles on the mistress, thus emphasizing the latter's contrasting *lack* of visual focus. Furthermore, the maid is shown calmly speaking, carrying out her commission as she pushes the "disturbance" into the letter writer's space. At this loaded moment, the upper hand, so to speak, is the subordinate's. The letter she proffers, sparkling white and crisply edged, exerts a strong visual presence, adding authority to its bearer.[23] She seems to possess prior knowledge, perhaps gained through her role as go-between. But Vermeer leaves forever unrevealed whether the mistress's apprehension will indeed prove merely fleeting. This painting's statement, about the uncertainties of love and thus of life, looms large.

Vermeer again describes an interruption in *The Love Letter* (figs. 58, 51). Yet his perspective shifts. In fact, nearly every account of this painting begins by remarking on its most noticeable spatial device. A near, dark, slightly out-of-focus framework on three sides opens suddenly onto a recessed, bright, well-furnished room, with the mistress and maid at its heart. Such rich profusion within so small a canvas: *The Love Letter* constitutes a witty pictorial conceit. Beaming out from its center with unusual clarity, the mistress's pearl earring epitomizes the work's artistic preciosity, indeed reversing the monumental *Mistress and Maid*.

In *The Love Letter*, the three-sided framework, cropped well before reaching a floor line, implies our close proximity to the aperture. The section at right consists of a wall parallel to the picture plane, against which a chair faces us, and on whose seat lie haphazardly two piles of paper. The top sheet of one, covered with illegible musical notations, rises, as if blown by a movement of air. Opposite, on the left side, a wall or door angles inward, as we can see from the loosely delineated map—the same one that appears much more prominently in *Woman in Blue Reading a Letter* (fig. 54) and *Young Woman with a Cavalier* (fig. 53). And beyond the unseen threshold to the far room, a pair of women's slippers and a propped-up broom nearly close off the center foreground. This internal frame makes us sharply aware of being outside the space that the two women inhabit. Moreover, the perspective orthogonals along the map's receding edges lead to a vanishing point at front right, slightly above the chair finial, locating us more precisely in the dark anteroom.[24] Inside, the mistress had been strumming a lute, no doubt as an outlet for her amorous feelings. But now, having taken the letter, she reveals surprise through her tight grip on the instrument's neck, the quick upward turn of her head toward the maid, her open mouth and raised eyebrows. The maid, by contrast, stands tall and erect, her left arm akimbo, a pose usually reserved for men in Dutch art. A diagonal white sash adds to her confident, nearly cocky

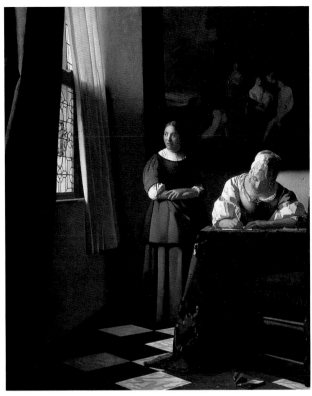

Fig. 58. Johannes Vermeer
The Love Letter, c. 1667–1670
Signed
Oil on canvas, 44 x 38.5 cm
Rijksmuseum, Amsterdam, no. SK-A-1595

Fig. 59. Johannes Vermeer
Lady Writing a Letter with her Maid, c. 1670-1672
Signed
Oil on canvas, 72.2 x 59.7 cm
National Gallery of Ireland, Dublin, cat. no. 4535

demeanor (as if she were a domestic, feminine version of a civic guardsman), and an exceptionally high, white headcovering further increases her stature. Looking down at her mistress's questioning face, she smiles, intimating that the lady's concern will prove unfounded. The calm sea represented in the large painting behind the two women supports this conclusion. Since the missive is sealed, however, we wonder how the maid could have discerned its contents. Plausibly, the absent gentleman arrived sooner than expected, gave both the letter and his confidences to the maid in person, and now conceals himself near the chair in the anteroom, so as to witness the unfolding of the lady's delight. His movement rustles the sheet of music. If this was Vermeer's intent, then the position of the vanishing point serves to elide the viewer with the proposed visitor, who waits, so to speak, in the wings.[25]

The diminutive intricacies and playful tone of *The Love Letter* compared with the grand human scale, minimal decor, and sense of portent in *Mistress and Maid* compel us to see these two pictures in a dialectical relationship. Representing a synthesis is *Lady Writing a*

Letter with Her Maid (figs. 59, 51), being about as much smaller than *Mistress and Maid* as it is larger than *The Love Letter*. "Synthesis" also applies to figural arrangements: in *Mistress and Maid* the women frame an empty center, in *The Love Letter* they nearly fill the center, and in *Lady Writing a Letter with Her Maid* the servant is at the exact center, the mistress close to the right frame.

Lady Writing a Letter with Her Maid, then, presents itself as the culminating example of Vermeer's epistolary scenes. A vivid illusion of inhabited cubic space, it shows a long, dark green curtain at left, withdrawn as if inviting entry. All the main elements can be grasped at a glance. Yet the scenario is among Vermeer's most challenging. An immense painting on the background wall depicts a biblical subject, The Finding of Moses (Exod. 2:1–10). What are we to make of this? Pictorial structure provides multiple hints. Throughout his work, Vermeer assigned unusual importance to axial relationships. Here, he vertically aligned a succession of motifs: the Madonna-like figure of Pharaoh's daughter holding the infant Moses in the painting above; the letter being written, situated midway; a leg of the chair in front of the table;

and finally, on the floor, the lit corner of what I take to be a partly open letter. Through this arrangement, the artist directs us to connect these aligned motifs thematically with the mistress. Pharaoh's daughter, known for her solicitousness, compassion, nobility, and independence, serves in part to characterize Vermeer's modern Dutchwoman through analogy. Relying on familiarity with the biblical account and other likely sources, including many Dutch paintings of the Finding of Moses, the analogy makes sense, especially given Vermeer's abiding interest in ideal feminine types. The maid, too, with her sentinel-like stance, is echoed in reverse by the biblical scene's sole standing figure, identifiable as Moses' "sister," a female relative who was sent to follow the child (Exod. 2:7–8). Vermeer evidently intended his audience to grasp a thematic connection here as well, since Moses' sister was to serve as a messenger, the anticipated role, too, of the letter writer's maid.[26]

The *Finding of Moses*, rising high on the wall, functions differently from the letter down on the floor. One sheet of it (or a wrapper) is crumpled. Two related objects, a round, bright red seal and a dark stick of sealing wax, lie nearby. A desire for tidy interpretation might make us wish for the maid to sweep away these things, and an earlier owner of the work actually had the seal and stick overpainted. They constitute, however, a fairly standard ploy, appealing to art lovers for whom speculation formed an enjoyable aspect of social conversation.[27] But in *Lady Writing a Letter with Her Maid* the role of the little still life on the floor is particularly difficult to ascertain. Was the mistress, shortly before, standing on our side of the table to open that letter? Or was it opened by whomever was sitting in the now-empty chair across from her—presumably a man? Why was the missive let drop? How did the stick of wax get there? Questions such as these, possibly unanswerable, might for that very reason inspire a multitude of diverse conclusions. The objects on the floor do indicate, however, a disturbance at odds with the calm demeanor of the lovely letter writer. They sound a note of urgency, enlivening the hushed interior, turning this scene into a sublime parlor mystery.

Gerard ter Borch's *An Officer Writing a Letter with a Trumpeter* (cat. 8), depicting an ace of hearts on the floor, and its pendant, *A Woman Sealing a Letter* (cat. 9), set up nearly as challenging a puzzle. But leaving that aside, we can easily imagine a plotted connection between the handsome ensign in the masculine scene and the pretty young woman in the companion piece, both of whom wait to deliver a letter. Ter Borch seems to imply that these two standing figures will meet one another on their way to transmit the letters entrusted to them. In

Vermeer's painting, too, we can construe the standing maid, who looks out the window, as visualizing amorous opportunities that the errand she awaits might offer.[28] In this scenario, the painter designed her wide-open gaze to convey longings in common with the mistress's, insofar as affairs of the heart are concerned. This hypothesis seems borne out in the ways Vermeer grants each woman greater autonomy than before, while still contriving ingeniously to pair them. One could argue that the mastery, novelty, and imagination so apparent in the earlier epistolary scenes evolve into something more profound in *Lady Writing a Letter with Her Maid*. But the latter's invention hardly seems possible without the daring explorations that preceded it.

Now to return more directly to artistic beauty. Vermeer's intentions can be partially gauged via the epistolary scenes' myriad intersections with his life.[29] Space allows mention of just a few. Regarding the paintings' amatory themes, John Michael Montias, seeking to explain Vermeer's demographically unusual marriage to Catharina Bolnes, has suggested that love might have been a strong motive; indeed, love, as we have seen, was thought to be a source of artistic inspiration.[30] The appeal for the painter of reading and writing women might also relate to his marriage. Catharina Bolnes came from a higher social class than he did, and she signed documents in an elegant hand. An interest in calligraphy can be discerned by comparing her fine penmanship with the "unadorned, workaday signature" of her highborn mother.[31] Vermeer's own mother, by contrast, was illiterate, and his sister, although she probably could read and write at an elementary level, wed a man who was completely illiterate at the time of their marriage.[32] And if we consider predilections as pertaining to both life and art, it bears observing that no male figure appears in Vermeer's epistolary scenes. Indeed, one of the most noticeable consistencies of his oeuvre is an artistic devotion to women. The surviving works picture about four times the average proportion of women to men in European painting of the era, including Dutch painting.[33] Men are not altogether absent from these scenes, of course, since a woman with a letter usually implies a man as either author or intended recipient of the depicted missive. Further, these paintings so strongly assert Vermeer's artistic individuality as to entail his own presence. Related to this, they contain many motifs corresponding to his documented household effects; relevant to *The Love Letter* alone are a yellow jacket trimmed with fur, two seascapes and a landscape, some lengths of gold-tooled leather on a wall, a green silk valance on a fireplace, and a wicker basket.[34] Vermeer's death inventory also lists twenty-five books, unfortunately with no titles mentioned. We nevertheless

Disciplining the Hand, Disciplining the Heart: Letter-Writing Paintings and Practices in Seventeenth-Century Holland

Ann Jensen Adams

Seventeenth-century genre paintings of letter writers and letter readers richly evoke two worlds of time and space: the thoughts, emotions, and locations of the depicted figures, and equally those of the absent intended recipient so palpably present in the minds of these pictured women and men. Such images captivate us precisely because we will never know the contents of these letters. While letters purport to speak the intimate thoughts of their author's minds, frustratingly for us, these figures and their letters remain silent. Such details as a dressing mirror (*fig. 30*) or the ace of hearts playing card dropped casually at the foot of a soldier (cat. 8) imply an intimate, even amorous, moment, yet we remain frustrated. Is the letter a family greeting, a gesture of friendship, or a declaration of love? If love, is it being sought or offered, rejected or declined? The paintings urge us to construct a story, complete a narrative. Indeed, the viewer is tempted to imagine him- or herself as the potential recipient or sender of the letter, a conversational partner with the pictured figure and the emotional connections implied by the missive. A shiver of potential pleasure—or disappointment—runs through the imaginative space of possibility between these exchanges, filled by the viewer's imagination.

Actual portraits of men often display letters held, sent, or most often received. Such portraits as Thomas de Keyser's portrait of the multitalented secretary to Prince Frederick Henry, *Portrait of Constantijn Huygens and a Messenger or Clerk* (see Sutton, Essay, *fig. 1*), or Michiel van Musscher's *Portrait of Thomas Hees*, the representative of the States General to Algiers, Tunis, and Tripoli with his nephews Andries and Johan Hees (see Sutton, Essay, *fig. 24*) inevitably suggest the transaction of business. Even when a couple are portrayed together, the letter is clearly addressed to the husband as, for example, Rembrandt's portrait of Jan Rijksen and Griet Jans (1633, Collection of Her Majesty Queen Elizabeth II, Buckingham Palace, London) or Abraham van den Tempel's *Married Couple* (1660, Museum of Fine Arts, Budapest). Similar portraits of women are rare.

In contrast, scores of genre paintings show young women who receive, read, and even write letters. These young ladies are imaginary, however, even when they may be modeled on a recognized sitter such as Gerard ter Borch's sister Gesina (cat. 5). Indeed, in many of ter Borch's paintings, there are few differences in either dress or demeanor between women who read and write letters, and those apparently engaged in transacting sex for money, a slippage that incites the pleasure of speculation about the boundaries of propriety (compare *figs. 10 & 11*). The woman in ter Borch's *Woman Writing a Letter* in the Mauritshuis (cat. 5) appears to be a fashionable young lady absorbed in composing a heartfelt missive; his similar but more conservatively dressed *Woman Holding a Letter* in Helsinki (cat. 10), however, is also drinking wine—alone: not the kind of thing in which a proper young woman would wish to be seen engaged. Such paintings arouse a tension in the viewer's imagination between the disciplined and excessive, the expression of friendship and amorous love. In the remainder of this essay I explore the sources and nature of this tension, by comparing these evocative paintings to what we know of contemporary values about, and practices of, letter writing.

Since classical antiquity, letters have been described as written conversation, as surrogates for face-to-face communication. The second-century Greek author Demetrius of Phaleron wrote that "everybody reveals his own soul in his letters. . . . A letter is designed to be the heart's good wishes in brief,"[1] while Seneca wrote to Lucilius, "I prefer that my letters should be just what my conversation would be if you and I were sitting in one another's company or taking walks together,— spontaneous and easy."[2] These and similar sentiments by ancient authors shaped the definition of the letter for sixteenth- and seventeenth-century men and women. Appending a Latin translation of Demetrius to his treatise on letter writing of 1591, and quoting Seneca, Justus Lipsius defined the letter as "a message of the mind to someone who is absent."[3] The popular letter-writing manuals written in vernacular Dutch that proliferated at the turn of the seventeenth century frequently refer to this tradition. In his *Ghemeene Seyndbrieven* (Common letters) published in Amsterdam in 1597, Heyman Jacobi defines the letter as "Een ontbiedinghe van d'eene mensch zyn sin de absent is" (a summoning of a person who is absent).[4] Similarly, in 1604 the art theorist Karel van Mander praises letters as "zwijzende boden" (silent messengers): "To the glory of colors we must add the art of writing in black and white. . . . Although they may be far apart, people can speak to one another by means of these silent messengers."[5] The seventeenth-century

63

scholar and prolific letter-writer Hugo Grotius turned this image on its head when his wife, Maria, was about to leave Paris for the Netherlands. Cutting short a letter to a friend, he explained that Maria, a "living letter," would be arriving soon.[6]

In spite of this weighty tradition, the private letter of the early modern period is something of an oxymoron if, by the private letter, we mean a written record of the spontaneous production of the innermost reaches of the soul. In practice, both the form of letters and the scripts in which they were written were increasingly codified or disciplined, much as other aspects of comportment and behavior were being restrained. Norbert Elias has described Desiderius Erasmus's *De civilitate morum puerilium* (On good manners for children) of 1530 as a turning point in the internalization of codes of behavior from deportment and table manners to behavior in the bedroom.[7] By the seventeenth century the language (if not the practice) of self-restraint had become an important part of the cultural vocabulary of the Northern Netherlands.[8] Not only was restraint of bodily demeanor being internalized, but public expressions of personal thoughts and emotions were also undergoing codification. The practices of letter writing were part of this process.

Three aspects of early modern letter writing provided forms of discipline, or restraint on expression. First, letters themselves were often produced and consumed by more individuals than their authors; letters often circulated in contexts that could dampen spontaneous expression of intimate sentiments. Second, as Peter Sutton describes in his essay, the seventeenth century witnessed a proliferation of letter-writing handbooks that codified for a popular audience the form these letters might take. Finally, calligraphy, or *schoonscrift* as it was called (literally, "beautiful writing"), became a widely recognized mark of culture taught in schools, displayed and promoted by manuals, and awarded in public competitions. All of these practices lent to the writing of letters a kind of cultural discipline, an internalization of restraint, against which these images of letter readers and writers could imaginatively play.

Letter writing and reading in the early modern period were practiced on a more public stage than is customary today:[9] they were experienced both orally and publicly as well as silently and privately. A substantial proportion of seventeenth-century men and women were literate to some degree, but fewer were able to compose a formal letter or craft letters in a fine hand. Many women in particular, while at the least trained to read and oversee household accounts, were unable to write with ease. Studies of the letter-writing practices of seventeenth-century Dutch women are only now being

undertaken; in his examination of approximately 2,300 letters written between 1540 and 1603 by some 650 Englishwomen, however, James Daybell found that many women did not write their own letters due to eccentric spelling, poor grammar, and atrocious handwriting.[10] Important letters were often dictated to a notary or a scribe, as we see pictured in several paintings of young men and young women by Gerard ter Borch (see, for example, cat. 8, *fig. 1*), resulting in a loss of confidentiality. As Erasmus put it in his treatise *De recta latini graecique sermonis pronuntiatione dialogus* (The right way of speaking Latin and Greek: a dialogue; 1528), "If you dictate verbatim, then it is goodbye to your privacy; and so you disguise some things and suppress others in order to avoid having an unwanted confidant. Hence, quite apart from the problem of the genuineness of the text, no open conversation with a friend is possible here."[11]

Letters entrusted to the mail, or even to private messengers, always ran the risk of being read along the way. In his highly popular letter-writing manual *Le Secrétaire à la mode* (The fashionable letter writer) of 1630, translated into Dutch in 1651 as *Fatsoenlicke zend-brief-schryver*, Jean Puget de la Serre warns that a writer should think twice about committing a secret to a letter because it might be exposed to the eyes of a reader for whom it was not intended. "For everybody knowes that it is not alwaies fitting to trust a secret to a Paper which may be lost, and fall into strangers hands."[12] Such concerns are reflected in the reassurance that Maria Tesselschade Roemers Visscher conveyed to Pieter Cornelisz. Hooft in a letter of July 1624, that he could safely send a reply to her through her brother who would protect Hooft's letter with one of his: "If it pleases Your Excellency to write, my brother will gladly deliver your letter with one of his wrapped around it."[13]

Once letters arrived, they might be read aloud, shown to others, or even published. Even when reading alone, individuals in the Middle Ages had voiced the texts they read.[14] This practice of voiced reading was still practiced by some in the seventeenth century as depicted, for example, in several paintings of elderly women reading the Bible: Rembrandt's *Old Woman Reading* (perhaps Rembrandt's mother as the Prophetess Hanna) of 1631 in the Rijksmuseum and Dou's paintings of similar old women in St. Petersburg and in Dresden. Well into the nineteenth century, the practice was still enough known that those who could not read silently might serve as an object of humor. When chided for reading a very private letter out loud, the farmer Colladan in Eugène Labiche's *La Cagnotte* (1864) responds: "If I read out loud, it's not for you, it's for me. . . . Whenever I don't read out loud . . . I don't understand what I'm reading."[15]

64

Male authors wrote letters fully aware of the tradition in which letters were shown to others, collected, and even published; at the least letters might be preserved by family members to be read by future generations.[16] One of Erasmus's correspondents informed him that "I do not merely lay up your letters among my literary treasures; I carry them round with me almost from door to door, because I think it good for my reputation that many people should be aware of my close relations with you."[17] Erasmus was annoyed when he discovered that a manuscript collection of some letters written in his youth had been found for sale by a friend in Italy.[18] He was not upset because his privacy had been invaded but because he had not had the opportunity to edit them. Indeed, the author later oversaw the publication of selections from his letters as early as 1519.[19]

Even in the seventeenth century, what we might consider private letters continued to be published. When Johannes Uytenbogaert wrote a particularly vivid letter to his wife from exile in Antwerp about recent political events, she asked his permission to have the letter printed for circulation.[20] The secretary to Prince Frederick Henry and prolific letter-writer Constantijn Huygens sent to friends Latin copies of his collection of poems, *Momenta desultoria* (Leisure moments) with handwritten dedications in the form of short poems. The second edition of this collection was printed both with Huygens's dedicatory poems and the personal thank-you letters written by his recipients.[21] After René Descartes's death, Elisabeth of Bohemia insisted to the French ambassador to Sweden, who had sorted through the philosopher's private papers, that her correspondence with Descartes not be published.[22] Nonetheless, as Paula Findlen has demonstrated, the fact and even the content of Elisabeth's correspondence seem to have been "reasonably well-known within the scholarly world in which learned women flourished."[23] Aware of these practices, any seventeenth-century letter writer may well have felt a certain amount of restraint in entrusting amorous emotions or intimate secrets to the written page.

Early modern men and women were also conscious that model books, of both letter texts and of script forms, discipline as they instruct. In his introduction to this catalogue, Peter Sutton describes the popular handbooks that offer directions for a broad variety of letter types. I turn, therefore, to the other manual genre that also flourished in this period in which personal writing of diaries and letters became increasingly popular:[24] the model books for the scripts in which these letters were written. These, too, most overtly those for children, provided through their discipline of the hand a discipline of the writer's character in the texts that were

Fig. 60. Gerard ter Borch
Paternal Admonition, c. 1654
Oil on canvas, 71 x 73 cm
Rijksmuseum, Amsterdam, SK-A-404

copied. Through the routine of imitating scripts, students internalized at once the shapes of the letters and the content of the aphorisms and quotations from classical authors that they reproduced. In his *De ratione studii puerilis* (On the method of instruction for children; 1523) written for Princess Mary Tudor and republished in the Northern Netherlands in the seventeenth century, Juan Luis Vives emphasized the disciplinary benefit of this internalization. Vives wrote: "Whilst we are writing, the mind is diverted from the thought of frivolous or improper objects. The lines which are just before the pupil for imitation should contain some weighty little opinion which it will be helpful to learn thoroughly, for by frequently writing out such, they will necessarily be fixed in the mind."[25] Clemens Perret's *Exercitatio alphabetica* (Alphabetical practice), first published by Christopher Plantin in Antwerp in 1569, offers models of scripts for the student to copy through moral maxims, in seven languages and their corresponding hands. A rather severe maxim in the English language reads: "Suke as the clearnesse of the eyes reioyseth the herte, so doeth a good name fede the bones. The care that harkeneth to the reformacyon of love, shall dwell among the wyse. He that refuseth to be refourmed, despiseth his own soule. God is mine onely trust."

The practice and prestige of *schoonschrift* reached a high point in the Netherlands during the first four decades of the seventeenth century. Calligraphy was

Fig. 61. Title page to Jan van de Velde, *Spieghel der schrijfkonste*, Rotterdam, 1605 (edition Amsterdam, first half 17th century). The Newberry Library, Chicago

admired as an art, widely appreciated and widely practiced, as suggested by the aphorism "Nil usu penna, sed arte" (It is not the use of the pen that matters, but the art with which it is employed). The painter and art theorist Karel van Mander called calligraphy "the art of the tenth Muse," and in his anthology of poems of twenty Dutch authors *Den Nederduytschen Helicon* (The Netherlandish helicon) of 1610 he placed professional calligraphers among the poets.[26] In his treatise on painting, van Mander describes the childhood precocity of the future painter Michiel van Miereveld by praising his ability to quickly master fine handwriting: "Michiel . . . was sent to school very young, and was so attentive and diligent in learning that he, still only a child of eight years old, he has made such progress in writing that he wrote better than any school master in the city of Delft." The script in which a letter was written was considered an important component of its content.

In the seventeenth century well-known calligraphers were celebrated in poetry and by painted and printed portraits, including Rembrandt's two well-known prints of a leading although slightly mad calligrapher, Lieven Willemsz. van Coppenol, of 1658.[27] Their works were avidly collected by artists and lovers of art. Number 250 in the inventory of Rembrandt's possessions made in 1656 is described as "Een dito [boeckie] met treffelijcke schriften" (One ditto [small book] with outstanding [examples of] calligraphy).[28] Friends penned original poems or familiar aphorisms in *album amicora* in a variety of scripts, such as the pages by Lieven van Coppenol and Anna Maria Schurman entered in the *album amicorum* of Jacob Heyblocq.[29] Individual sheets of calligraphy were even hung proudly beside paintings in Dutch homes. In

his investigation of the inventories of Delft houses, John Michael Montias found numerous examples of individual sheets of fine writing, particularly by the celebrated Delft schoolmaster Felix van Sambix. framed and displayed on the walls.[30]

The high status and broad popularity of *schoonschrift* are attested by the numerous calligraphy contests held beginning at the end of the sixteenth century. On Christmas Eve 1589 a number of writing masters competed in Rotterdam for the so-called Prix de la Plume Couronnée (The Crowned Quill Prize). The competition was won by three of the leading writing masters of the day. The first prize, a golden quill, went to the Delft schoolmaster Felix van Sambix, second to Salomon Hendrix, and third to the young Jan van de Velde who would go on to publish the most sumptuous writing books of the century, including his celebrated *Spieghel der schrijfkonste* (Mirror of the art of writing; Rotterdam, 1605; *fig. 61*).[31]

Writing was valued not so much because it was a skill mastered by a few but because it was an activity in which skill and discrimination were exercised, a skill with an elaborate and widely recognized code in its forms alone. The script in which a letter was written carried very specific social associations that located the writer and reader within a matrix of coded social relationships. Puget de la Serre wrote that the letter "should not tire the Readers eyes, but be written so fair that it may delight the sight with looking upon it."[32] In such a society it would have been difficult to produce letters that could have been understood and judged outside this context. Even those viewers who themselves had not mastered a variety of hands, or who may not have understood the precise associations of each script, would nonetheless have recognized that such codes were being cited.

Well-educated letter writers occasionally expressed self-consciousness about the quality of their handwriting. In a letter dated December 10, 1635, the Dutch humanist, poet, and playwright P. C. Hooft wrote to his friend Justus Baak that he had changed his handwriting, but apologized for not having yet mastered the forms of the italic. He explained: "the letter that speaks must first be justified. Its changing comes forth from two reasons. Because the way the Dutch [Gothic] script has been made has always displeased me. I much prefer the Latin or round Italian, which also goes fast. That I write so very badly is clear to my eyes. But time will teach me, as the saying goes."[33] In a refreshingly breezy letter to her brother Constantijn, later to become the secretary to Prince Frederick Henry, Constance Huygens writes: "I ask that you forgive my poor handwriting; it is due to my great haste."[34]

Between the middle of the sixteenth and the mid–seventeenth centuries, a substantial number of manuals published in the Netherlands provided both directions and models for the improvement of handwriting skills.[35] Presenting sample pages in a variety of alphabetic scripts, these ranged from schoolbooks to luxury editions for collectors and connoisseurs.[36] They responded both to the increased interest in writing in general and to an awareness that the form of the script in which a text was produced was highly codified, and as eloquent as the language, linguistic structure, and content of the text itself.

Renaissance handwritten scripts, like their counterparts in printed typefaces, may be roughly divided into four categories: the Gothic, or black letter, of which Textura and Fraktur are variants; a Gothic cursive known as Civilité; the all-capital roman; and the rounded italic (*fig. 62*).[37] In the seventeenth century each of these had specific associations with languages and textual genres and were employed following well-established hierarchies. Producers of texts, from the authors of intimate letters to publishers of popular books, employed these scripts with an awareness of the educational level and social position of the author and intended readers. The form of a script thus self-consciously positioned the author, the text, and the reader within a widely understood artistic and social language.

Seventeenth-century handwritten scripts are best understood in the context of the printed tradition. The oldest form employed for printed books was the Gothic black letter, which for manuscripts had replaced the rounded Carolingian in northern Europe in the twelfth century.[38] Gutenberg's Bible, for example, was set in this type.[39] Its thick and dark, closely packed, vertical strokes produced words with a strong physical presence on the page. Even after the roman typeface had achieved wide currency in Italy from the 1470s, Gothic continued to be the predominant script in the Netherlands until the seventeenth century. In the first Dutch translation of book 4 of Sebastiano Serlio's treatise on architecture (1639), Pieter Coecke van Aelst replaced Serlio's chapter 13 on heraldic ornament with his own discussion of letter design and two pages of roman letters designed by himself.[40] He explains that he has used Gothic, or "Brabant letters," for the text, however, "so that ordinary people can read it more easily," although he himself preferred the roman typeface.[41]

In the seventeenth century, the Gothic continued to be used for popular texts appealing to the broadest possible audience, from the Dutch translation of the Bible authorized by the States General after the Synod of Dort and published in 1637 to such public broadsides as

Fig. 62. Photomontage of four scripts from Jan van de Velde, *Spieghel der schrijfkonste* (Mirror of Calligraphy), Rotterdam, 1605
Textura (upper left); Dutch Civilité (upper right); Roman (lower left); Italic (lower right).

the announcement of the sale of Rembrandt's drawings and prints of 1658.[42] The Gothic also continued to be employed for popular texts written in the vernacular. Comedies such as Hooft's *Whare-nar*, a Dutch translation of Plautus's *Kluchtighe comedie. Aulularia* (Farcical comedy, "Aulularia") of 1617, and Gerbrand Adriaensz. Bredero's comic work, to name just a few, were published in Gothic typeface.[43]

At the same time, the upper- and lowercase roman was replacing the Gothic for the publication of more serious texts, such as histories and published tragedies.[44] Certain elements of popular culture were still preserved in the appearance of texts, however, as different voices were printed in different typefaces.[45] The 1636 edition of Vondel's comic-tragedy (tragedy with a happy ending) *Het Pascha; or, the Rescue of the Children of Israel from Egypt* of 1612, for example, employs different typefaces to distinguish the social location of the voices they embody. Here the text is in roman but the voices of the choruses that interrupt it are in the older Gothic type.[46]

Italic, also called chancery, had risen to prominence in Italy in the late fifteenth century, when it became the favored script of the papal chancery in Rome. It was based on the clear, upright, rounded script known as humanist *antiqua*, and when written quickly became slanted, attenuated, and cursive. The italic came to be associated with the prestige of the Latin language and humanist learning, while the black letter or Gothic remained employed for popular texts and the roman for more serious texts in the vernacular.[47]

Based on the conventions of printed texts, alphabetic

forms of handwriting were also codified, each with a different intended impact on its readers. In his *Lettre défensive, pour l'art de bien escrire* (In defense of the art of writing; Rotterdam, 1599) Jan van de Velde wrote that "the master penman . . . will know that some are moved by italic and Spanish letters, others by letters of state or business."[48] That such differentiation was fundamental is indicated by the entry on *ars scriptoria*, or the art of writing, in Johannes Amos Comenius's first illustrated and highly successful grammar school textbook, *Orbis sensualium pictus* (Picture of the visible world; Nuremberg, 1658), whose publication in a bilingual Latin and German edition Comenius directed from Amsterdam.[49] Its typography was set in three different faces: the Latin text was printed in roman in both lowercase and capitals, while the words corresponding to the objects numbered in the illustration were set in italics. The German translation was printed in black letter or Fraktur. Similar distinctions are made in an anonymous bilingual compilation of musical treatises intended for use in a secondary school (the Latin school or Gymnasium of Harderwijk) by both teachers and pupils published in Leiden in 1605. The *Brevia mvsicae rvdimenta latino belgicae / corte onderwijsinghe van de Mvsike* presents the same text printed in Latin and Dutch on facing pages. Latin is displayed in an italic typeface with roman titles; the Dutch on the facing page is set in lowercase roman with Gothic titles.[50]

In the history of these texts can be traced both the high value placed on a knowledge of letter forms and the breadth of the public that would have understood their values and codes. Gerard Mercator, best known today for inventing the system by which the three dimensions of the globe may be represented by the two dimensions of a

map, published the first *exemplaer boeck*, or calligraphic model book, to be produced in the Netherlands. His *Literarum latinarum, quas italicas, cursoriasque vocant, scribendarum ratio* (Method of writing Latin letters, called italic and cursive; Louvain, 1540), printed from woodcut blocks and in a vertical format, gave all the information a designer would need to know for creating an italic script.[51] These include a discussion of writing implements, how to hold the pen, and detailed instructions on the creation of letters in the italic style. In addition, the directions themselves are printed in an italic script, thus serving as an example book of the instructions they outline. This volume was not so much a handbook on handwriting for a general audience as a manual addressed to the designers of technical publications, maps, and globes, such as those Mercator himself was publishing.[52]

Mercator's book was followed by Clemens Perret's *Exercitatio alphabetica* published in Antwerp in 1569.[53] In contrast to Mercator's volume written for professionals, Perret's was a brilliant showpiece designed to appeal to collectors and connoisseurs. Its subtitle stresses the visual dimension of his work, its "rare ornamentation, shading, and recession, derived from imagery and architecture."[54] It was the first example book produced from engraved copperplates, and it was also the first to display seven different scripts, each corresponding to a different European language: Latin, Italian, French, Spanish, English, German, and Dutch.[55] Jodocus Hondius in the Northern Netherlands followed Perret's book with his *Theatrum artis scribendi* (Theater of the art of writing), published in Amsterdam in 1594. To the seven language scripts published by Perret, Hondius added Hebrew and Greek, and included sample pages designed by a variety

Opposite left: Fig. 63. Instructions for holding the pen from David Roelands' *T'magazin oft' pac-huys der loffelycker penn-const…* [Vlissinghem? or Amsterdam] 1616.
The Newberry Library, Chicago

Opposite right: Fig. 64. Page 15 from Gesina ter Borch's *De papiere Lauwekrans*, c. 1652, pen and watercolor (Amsterdam, Rijksprentenkabinet) inv. no. A 1890/1952

Fig. 65. Maria Strick, *Tooneel der loflijcke schrijfpen … int licht gebracht door Maria Strick… Ghesneden door Hans Strick* [Delft?] 1607, alphabet and text of Latin hand
The Newberry Library, Chicago

of different calligraphers, including Felix van Sambix who had won the Golden Quill in Rotterdam in 1589.[56] The calligraphic texts of both Perret's and Hondius's books are embellished with ornamented borders that recollect sculpted architectural frames.

In 1605 appeared the largest and most sumptuous of these editions, Jan van de Velde's *Spieghel der schrijfkonste* (*fig. 61*).[57] Designed entirely by van de Velde and masterly engraved by Simon Frisius—himself a writing master of some note—it offers alphabets and texts in the now customary seven languages and at least fourteen corresponding styles. It was divided into three parts: the first presents Dutch, French, German, and English, for speed (merchants, notaries, secretaries); the second, "Thresor Literaire," shows the cursive Latin, Italian, and Spanish; the third, "Fondement-Boeck," is a treatise and manual on how alphabets are formed. It also includes pages illustrating two different ways to hold the pen for different alphabets.

Although it contains much practical information, van de Velde's book above all celebrates the art of the pen both visually and in its text. Unlike the architectural borders of Perret's and Hondius's works, for example, van de Velde's pages are embellished with elaborate ornaments and even figures made entirely with the pen—often in a single stroke. In some cases these ornaments threaten to overpower their text; an opening page reads "Vive la Plume" (Long live the quill [feather pen]) in handwriting so elaborate that it nearly obscures the text it inscribes. In addition to the frequently moralizing texts of his predecessors, van de Velde includes texts dedicated to well-known men both ancient and contemporary and includes examples of the work of the well-known fellow calligrapher van Sambix, the artist

Hendrick Goltzius, and van de Velde's own father, Hans.

Published to appeal to wealthy and influential collectors, van de Velde's book was unprecedented in its ambition and apparently its price. In 1617 the author felt he could ask the remarkable sum of 100 guilders for his book, astonishing in comparison with the annual income of a master carpenter or bricklayer that was not more than about 250 guilders a year in the first half of the seventeenth century.[58] This is also an extraordinary contrast with the wholesale price that Perret received from the Antwerp publisher Christopher Plantin in 1570 for his manual: 100 guilders for 80 copies.[59] The *exemplaer boeck* was apparently a popular genre, for an increasing number of different volumes were published, including another by van de Velde in the same year, his *Deliciae variarum, insigniumque scripturarum* (The pleasures of diverse, eminent scripts), and nine different books by the author in all.[60] David Roelands's *T'magazin oft' pac-huys der loffelycker penn-const* (The warehouse or the storehouse of the praiseworthy art of the pen) of 1616 also combines both instruction (*fig. 63*) with examples of virtuosity in handling the pen.

While certainly in the minority, women were not excluded from learning and practicing this fine art, perhaps because it could be undertaken in the privacy of their home.[61] Jodocus Hondius included two pages by his sister Jacquemyne among the specimens of works by well-known calligraphers in his *Theatrum artis scribendi* of 1594. The entry by Anna Maria van Schurman in Jacob Heyblocq's *album amicorum*, and the pages of the charming illustrated manuscript "De papiere Lauwekrans" by Gerard ter Borch's sister Gesina both evidence exquisitely skilled hands (*fig. 64*).[62] Of even greater renown was Maria Strick, the schoolmistress of a French school in Rotterdam and author of several writing books with examples of her remarkable work. Her *Tooneel der loflijcke schrijfpen* (Theater of the praiseworthy pen) published in Delft in 1607, like van de Velde's larger *Spieghel*, is elaborately embellished with pen ornaments (*fig. 65*).[63] She subsequently authored and designed her *Christelycke ABC* (Christian ABC; Rotterdam, 1611), *Schat oft Voorbeelt ende Verthooninge Van Verscheyden Geschriften* (Treasury or models and presentations of various writings; Rotterdam, 1618), and the *Fonteyne des levens* (Fountain of life; Rotterdam, 1624), all of whose pages were engraved by her husband, Hans Strick.

Maria Strick's outstanding skill was publicly recognized when she was awarded second prize in a handwriting competition held in The Hague early in August 1620.[64] The rather querulous winner of the first place, Joris de Carpentier, complained of Strick's award, however. He was upset that she received her prize on the basis of her excellence in the Italian scripts alone. De Carpentier seems to have been galled that Strick was able to boast that she could write the Italian hand better than he and argued that the awards should have been based on all-round calligraphic ability, rather than on one particular category. In a letter to an apparent juror, he asks that Maria be challenged to another contest for the extraordinary sum of 300 gulden, in which judgment will be based on all scripts.

At the same time that calligraphy was being admired and purchased by connoisseurs, a broad spectrum of students was exposed to at least the rudiments of the art. In 1591 the Barsingerhorn schoolmaster Dirck Adriaensz. Valcooch wrote a manual for schoolmasters in which he praised calligraphy: "Over many arts, it t he crown must wear—O you young ones, take your pleasure there."[65] Valcooch devoted several chapters to "schrijven te leeren." He recommended that students practice their writing every Saturday to prepare themselves to compete in writing contests to be held by the schoolmaster four times a year.[66] The teaching of handwriting in the French and Latin schools of the Netherlands became extensive enough to be attacked by the mathematician Martin Wentsel, who in 1599 argued that too much importance was being placed on this art over mathematics.[67]

Valcooch mentions example sheets that were to be made by the schoolmaster and perhaps individual engraved examples collected by him.[68] An increasing number of relatively inexpensive model books directed toward a student audience also began to be published. Some of these were not engraved, but published with set typography, which dramatically reduced their price.[69] The title page of *Eenen nieuwen ABC of materi-boeck* (A new

ABC or copy book), written by Dirck Coornhert and published by Willem Silvius in 1564, recommends it to "boys and girls who have no opportunity to go to masters who can handle the pen with style."[70] Typical of these books, it was set in Civilité, or *geschreven letter* (handwritten letter), a Gothic cursive, the older and more widely read typeface and script, in contrast to the italic associated with Latin. Clemens Perret, who in 1569 had published his *Exercitatio alphabetica* discussed above, also published an engraved example book for a broader audience in 1571 that, following the model of its more costly counterpart, presented a variety of scripts, each associated with a different language. The full title of his *Eximiae peritiae alphabetum* advertises it as "Alphabets of exceptional skill, containing numerous writing exemplars and as many different scripts, shown in seven languages. A booklet as useful as it is necessary for all educated persons and also young people who enjoy practicing the art of penmanship. For in studying and copying it beginners will not only acquire greater proficiency in this art, but they will also gain perfect standards for writing similar characters in these languages."[71]

The topos that the traces of the hand are the most personal mark of the individual goes back to classical antiquity.[72] In the prefatory sonnet that Karel van Mander wrote celebrating the calligraphy of Jan van de Velde for the latter's *Spieghel der schrijfkonste*, van Mander praises the naturalness of the master's hand, issuing as if from nature.[73] Nonetheless, at the turn of the seventeenth century, learned script—the disciplined hand—was actually highly impersonal. As Walter Melion has demonstrated, the "naturalness" so praised by van Mander was not a unique, personal mark, but the ability to impersonate perfectly the hands of many other masters. Indeed, this was precisely the skill that de Carpentier wished to have recognized in his complaint about the outcome of the writing contest of 1620. A second poem published in van de Velde's *Spieghel*, written by M. V. Compostel in praise of van de Velde's calligraphy, reads: "Not Somer's person alone, which is still revered, nor Hesel's, nor Perret's should live in you, but Beauchêsne's and Curione's, too, would be exalted, as would others who once thrived, for you alone could imitate them all."[74] Van de Velde himself insisted in his *Deliciae variarum, insigniumque scripturarum* of 1604–5, "virtuosity lies in the ability to imitate multiple hands." In his *Lettre défensive* of 1599, van de Velde had similarly insisted that,

> just as those who teach arithmetic cannot rely simply on two or three rules, but must have a thorough grounding in all the rules, and those who teach French cannot know it only after a fashion, but must grasp it completely in order to render it cogently, so too the master penman

Catalogue

List of artists

DIRCK HALS

(Haarlem 1591–1656 Haarlem)

The family of Dirck and his eldest brother, the famous portrait painter Frans Hals, emigrated from Antwerp after it fell to the Spanish in 1585. The first evidence of their presence in Haarlem was Dirck's baptism there on March 19, 1591. Their father was a cloth dresser. Dirck may have learned the rudiments of painting from Frans, who became a master in the guild in 1610. Their middle brother, Joost, whose work is unidentified, also was recorded as a painter. Dirck, like Frans, lived most of his life in Haarlem; however, in 1641–43 and 1648 (and probably during the intervening years) he was a resident of Leiden. Dirck was a member of the corporalship of the St. George's civic guard in Haarlem from 1618 to 1624. Frans was also a member of the guard, and both brothers belonged to the rhetorician's society known as the De Wijngaertranken (The Vine Tendrils). In 1620 or 1621 Dirck married Agnieta Jansdr. in Haarlem, and they subsequently baptized seven children in the Reformed Church. The engraver Jan van de Velde (1593–1641) was a friend; he attended the baptism of one of Dirck's children and entered a sworn testimony that Dirck was owed twenty-four guilders in "wages" by another engraver, Willem Outgertsz. Ackersloot. This suggests that Dirck was employed by other artists before he became a master in the Haarlem guild in 1627. The following year, Samuel Ampzing made flattering reference to both Hals brothers in his chronicle of the city of Haarlem (see below). In 1629 Dirck acquired paintings at a local auction run by the painter Frans Pietersz. de Grebber (1572–1649), which required surety promised by Frans. A lucrative sideline for artists during this period was dealing in paintings; Dirck organized two painting auctions, in 1634 (with the printmaker Cornelis van Kittensteyn) and in 1635 (with the local still-life painter Franchois Elout). Among the works offered were paintings by Dirck and Frans Hals, as well as by Salomon van Ruysdael, Jan van Goyen, and Judith Leyster. Dirck also was associated with the Amsterdam art dealer and painter Pieter Jansz. van den Bosch and collected the proceeds from the latter's auctions. He moved to Leiden in 1641, but the following June his possessions were confiscated for nonpayment of rent. He nonetheless was probably still in the city in 1649 when he was recorded as living on the Noordeinde. On that occasion his goods were again confiscated, suggesting that Dirck had frequent financial problems. When he died in May 1656, his family was not required to pay burial tax to the city of Leiden, indicating that he had moved back to Haarlem, probably seven years earlier.

Hals was a painter of genre scenes usually on a small scale and often of merry company or domestic subjects. His works were commended by Samuel Ampzing in 1628 (*Beschrijvinge ende Lof der Stad Haerlem*) for his "neat little figures," and he also won the praise of his contemporary T. Scrivelius (*Harlemius, Ofte om beter te seggen, De eerste stichtinghe der Stadt Haerlem* [Haarlem, 1648]) for being "very fine and pure in small pieces and figures." Notable influences on Hals's syle were the works of Willem Buytewech (1591–1624) and Esaias van de Velde (1587–1630). In the late 1620s Dirck collaborated with the architectural painter Dirck van Delen (1605–1671), for whom he supplied the figures. Dirck's son, Anthonie (1621–1691), was a painter of portraits and genre scenes in Amsterdam. Several engravers reproduced Dirck's works, including Cornelis van Kittensteyn, Salomon Savery, and Gillis van Scheyndal.

–PCS

Literature: Plietzsch 1960, pp. 26–27; Philadelphia/Berlin/London 1984, pp. 204–7; Haarlem/Worcester 1993, pp. 256–77.

Cat. 1.
DIRCK HALS
Woman Reading a Letter by Candlelight
Signed lower right: *D HALS*
Oil on panel, 22 x 29 cm
Accademia Carrara, Bergamo, cat. no. 565

Provenance: Carlo Longhi, Milan; bequest of Count Guglielmo Lochis to the City of Bergamo, 1859 (as Cornelis Dusart), in the museum since 1866.

Literature: Bode 1883, p. 125 (as Dirck Hals); Julianne Harms, "Judith Leyster: Ihr Leben und ihr Werk," *Oud Holland* 44 (1927), no. 23 (as Judith Leyster); C. Hofstede de Groot, "Schilderiijen van Judith Leyster," *Oud Holland* 46 (1929), p. 26 (as Dirck Hals); Sutton, in exh. cat. Philadelphia/Berlin/London 1984, p. lxv n. 84; Francesco Rossi, *Accademia Carrara. Catalogo dei dipinti sec. XVII–XVIII* (Milan, 1989), p. 112, ill., p. 113, inv. no. 565, ill.; F. Fox Hofrichter, *Judith Leyster* (Doornspijk, 1989), p. 76, no. D6, ill.; exh. cat. Haarlem/Worcester 1993, p. 277 n. 1; Guido Jansen, Bert W. Meijer, and Paola Squellati Brizio, *Repertory of Dutch and Flemish Paintings in Italian Public Collections,* vol. 2, *Lombardy (A–L)* (Florence, 2001), p. 234, no. 400, ill.

Viewed three-quarter length, a woman seated at a table reads a letter by the light of a candle. Smiling, she wears an apron and a cap and places her hand casually on her hip as she reads. On the table to the right are three books, one of which stands on its end. The light casts a large shadow of her form on the back wall.

Although the painting was misattributed to Cornelis Dusart in the nineteenth century and to Judith Leyster by Julianne Harms (1927), it was correctly recognized as a work by Dirck Hals by Wilhelm Bode (1883) and even bears the artist's signature. It is one of a group of paintings that Dirck Hals executed in the late 1620s and early 1630s that pioneered the letter theme in genre painting. While most of his paintings are of merry company subjects, sometimes situated in large and extravagantly outfitted banqueting halls painted by Dirck van Delen, Dirck Hals also painted more intimate and distinctly unpretentious domestic scenes of women and children in the home. As early as 1628 the chronicler of Haarlem, Samuel Ampzing, praised Dirck in his *Beschrijvinge ende Lof der Stadt Haarlem*, for his "neat little figures." Here Dirck addresses the letter subject in a spare and sparsely decorated interior that is complemented by a direct and unembellished painting style. Although it is a

Fig. 1. Dirck Hals
Woman Reading a Letter by Candlelight
Monogrammed and dated: *1636*
Oil on panel, 23.5 x 20 cm
Sale, Amsterdam, "G. à Paris," Muller, June 19, 1920, no. 18, ill.

domestic setting, the woman is not dealing with children, family, or household matters but relaxes with her reading, while at her side are books, the attributes of learning. Dirck Hals had certainly observed the domestic life of women at firsthand; he and his wife, Agnietje Jans, had seven children between 1621 and 1635, and he painted charming pictures of women ministering to children (see *Woman Cleaning a Child's Hair by Lamplight*, signed and dated 1631, P. and N. de Boer Foundation, Amsterdam; ill. in exh. cat. Haarlem/Worcester 1993, no. 27) and children at play (dated 1631?, Sterling and Francine Clark Art Institute, Williamstown, Massachusetts, nos. 756, 757). But here he celebrates without comedy (compare cat. 2) or condescension the quiet enjoyment that a woman may take in written private correspondence and the life of the mind. Among the paintings that Hals and his partner, Cornelis van Kittensteyn, offered for auction at the Basterpijp Tavern on the Smedestraat in Haarlem in 1634 was a painting by Dirck described as *A Woman Reading*, valued at eighteen guilders.

The present work is similar in conception to the scene of a smiling woman reading a letter by candlelight (the light source in that case is hidden) in a painting signed and dated 1636 by Dirck Hals that sold in Amsterdam in 1920 (*fig. 1*). By situating the letter theme in these two paintings at night with an oil lamp or candle, he explores dramatic lighting effects that cast looming shadows on the back wall, enlarging the women's form and by implication the simple act of reading a letter. Compare also the similar lighting effects in the maternal scene dated 1631 in the P. and N. de Boer Foundation mentioned above. Only two years later, Judith Leyster would follow him in exploring dramatic nocturnal lighting in small-scale domestic scenes (see her *Woman Sewing by Candlelight*, National Gallery of Ireland, Dublin, no. 468, and its pendant, formerly in the Schloss Collection, *Woman with a Child by Candlelight*, initialed and dated 1633).

The nocturnal setting for the letter subject was often associated with devoted scholars and people of letters working into the night. However, the depictions of night schools as expressions of earnest education and scholars working by candlelight as embodiments of the Aristotelian ideal of practice were codified only later by Gerard Dou and his followers (see J. A. Emmens, "Natuur, Onderwijzing en Oefening. Bij een drieluik van Gerrit Dou," *Album Discipulorum J. G. van Gelder* [Utrecht, 1963], pp. 123–36). In later works by Dou's pupil, Frans van Mieris, the night is again the preferred time for letters, their conception and writing (see cats. 21–23).

—PCS

Cat. 2.
DIRCK HALS
Seated Woman with a Letter, 1633
Signed and dated on the foot warmer: *DHals 1633*
Oil on panel, 34.2 x 28.3 cm
Philadelphia Museum of Art: The John G. Johnson
Collection, 1917, J#434

Provenance: Acquired by John G. Johnson before 1913.

Exhibition: Philadelphia/Berlin/London 1984, cat. 46,
pl. 12; Frankfurt 1993, no. 35, ill.

Literature: Philadelphia, Johnson, cat. 1913, vol. 2, p. 66;
de Jongh 1967, p. 52, fig. 38; Philadelphia, Johnson, cat.
1972, p. 44, ill.; exh. cat. Amsterdam 1976, p. 121, fig. 25a;
Wieseman 2002, p. 60, fig. 15.

A lady in a blue jacket, gold skirt, pearl earrings, wide
white collar, and long narrow apron arranges herself
comfortably in a chair. One red slipper on a foot warmer
peeps out from her skirt. Smiling, she holds a letter in
her left hand while she drapes her arm over the back
of the ladder-back chair in which she sits. At the left is
a leaded window with curtains, and at the back right a
molded doorjamb, a second chair, and a painting in a
black ebony frame with gilt borders depicting a calm
seascape. In the 1913 catalogue of the Johnson collection
by W. R. Valentiner, this painting was described as "in the
manner of Simon de Vlieger," although it is scarcely
visible beyond its adumbration of a panoramic marine
with overcast sky, still water, low horizon, and sailing
vessels.

The present work is dated 1633 and is one of several
paintings by Dirck Hals that seem to be among the first
true genre scenes involving letters. The painting *Woman
Tearing up a Letter* in the Landesmuseum, Mainz (Sutton
essay, *fig. 2*) is dated two years earlier, 1631, while the
nocturnal painting of a woman reading a letter from
the museum in Bergamo (cat. 1) may predate that
picture. Another later example of Dirck Hals's letter
themes in a nocturnal setting is *Woman Reading a Letter
by Candlelight,* signed and dated 1636 (see cat. 1, *fig. 1*),
which like the present work has an upright composition
but is focused on a three-quarter-length image. As with
the comfortably inclined and unbuttoned lady who looks
out affably at the viewer here, the two ladies in the night
scenes seem to enjoy the news they have received. The
casual pose of the lady in the present work, with her arm
slung over the chair back, is one that Dirck's brother,
Frans, employed for his famously spontaneous portraits.

We cannot know the contents of these letters, but as
Eddy de Jongh (1967) first observed in discussing the

Fig. 1. Engraved illustration entitled "Als zijt hij vert,
noyt uyt het hert" from Jan Harmensz. Krul, *Minne-beelden*
(Amsterdam, 1640), p. 2
Library, Faculty of Arts, Utrecht University

present and several related works, paintings-within-
paintings were a traditional device used by artists in
the seventeenth century to comment on the subjects of
their genre scenes. The seascape in the background of the
present work may therefore have a bearing on the letter
theme. The conceit of likening human emotions to the
changeable moods of the sea is as old as literature.
Queuing in a long line of poets, the seventeenth-century
Dutch poet Jan Hermansz. Krul, provided a widely
known example of this trope in his *Minne-beelden,* which
was illustrated with a vessel under full sail piloted by
cupid with a lover in the bow, under the motto "Al zijt
ghy vert, noyt uit het hert" (Although you are far away,
you are in my heart; *Minne-beelden: toegepast de lievende
ionckheyt* [Amsterdam, 1640], pp. 2–3; first cited by de
Jongh 1967, p. 52). The appended verses (see Sutton
essay) explain that love is as changeable as the sea. The
glassy marine at the back and the calm seascape behind
the smiling woman in the candlelit scene of 1636 offer
a potential metaphor for the contentment of the letter's
recipient. We can understand the need for reassurance
when at any given moment in the seventeenth century
such a large proportion of the male population of
Holland was at sea and exposed to its dangers. In
seventeenth century poetry by Jacob van Someren and
others, women often write or receive passionate letters
from lovers at sea (see Schotel 1903, pp. 188–89). In
the painting in Mainz (Sutton, Introduction, *fig. 2*), by
contrast, the woman tears up the letter and sways slightly,

Cat. 6.
GERARD TER BORCH
Officer Reading a Letter with a Trumpeter, c. 1657–58
Oil on canvas, 37.5 x 28.5 cm
Gemäldegalerie Alte Meister, Staatliche
Kunstsammlungen Dresden, inv. no. 1833

Provenance: Royal Saxon Collection, inv. 1722, no. 525, as Gabriel Metsu.

Literature: Hofstede de Groot, vol. 5 (1912), no. 27; E. Plietzsch, *Gerard ter Borch* (Vienna, 1944), p. 22; Dresden, Gemäldegalerie, cats. 1930, 1956 and 1992, no. 1883; Gudlaugsson 1959–60, vol. 1, p. 114-115, pl. 130, vol. 2, p. 144, no. 130, ill.; exh. cat. Frankfurt 1993, p. 150, ill. fig. 10.1.

An officer with reddish blond hair, wearing a broad-brimmed gray hat, gray trousers, and cuirass, with decorative ribbons at his knees and cuffs, sits in profile reading a letter. Before him stands a trumpeter, also in profile, waiting in a striped blue costume with rider's boots, sword, and his instrument slung over his back, holding his ample fur hat respectfully before him. Between them is a simple wooden table, beyond which sits another soldier with long hair and a steel gorget. The darkened interior is ill defined, but the rustic furnishings and shards of a clay pipe on the floor suggest a guardroom or other basic lodging.

Ter Borch addressed the subject of letters read and written by military men repeatedly (see cats. 7, 8; cat. 8, *fig. 1*, and Sutton essay, *fig. 4*). In the case of the pendants joining a man and a woman exhibited here (see cats. 8 & 9), the suggestion is that the correspondence is amorous in nature, but in the present work it is unclear whether the officer has received a personal message or a professional dispatch. His relaxed, even bemused expression implies that it may be the former. However, the painting has been assumed to be the pendant to the painting exhibited here from Warsaw (cat. 7), which also depicts a seated officer, in that case writing, with a standing trumpeter again in a similar costume with fur hat and employing a complementary design. From a stylistic point of view, the two panels of nearly the same dimensions share a monumental aspect, concentrating on a few full-length figures of comparable scale arranged around a table, executed with a relatively dark palette with bright color accents and comparably assured brushwork, suggesting that they were executed at about the same time, in the mid to later 1650s. Moreover, they were both part of royal Saxon collections in the eighteenth century. Thus they have been assumed in

he past to be companion pieces. Even Gudlaugsson (1959–60, vol. 2, p. 144), who exposed the fact that many works by ter Borch originally conceived as independent paintings were wed as companions by later collectors, especially in the eighteenth century, thought that the two works might have been designed by the artist as pendants. Not only do the designs complement one another and many of the same figures and furnishings recur, but their subjects could be regarded as a progressive narrative: the writing and receiving of official military orders or reports. However, as the authors of the exhibition in Frankfurt in 1993 (p. 150) observed, there are subtle differences, for example, in the trumpeters' costumes and appearance, which suggest that he is not the same courier. They questioned whether a narrative was intended between the two works or if ter Borch was simply exercising his custom of closely varying favored themes and designs.

The officer depicted here was a model that ter Borch favored, especially in the 1660s (compare Gudlaugsson 1959–60, nos. 169, 192, and 219), and may be Moses ter Borch. Gudlaugsson lists five copies of the picture (his nos. 130a–e), testifying to its popularity, and Johannes Lingelbach copied the figures here depicted in a military scene in the Gemeentemuseum, Arnhem.

–PCS

Cat. 7. (Exhibited in Dublin only)
GERARD TER BORCH
An Officer Writing a Letter
Oil on panel, 41 x 28.5 cm
National Museum, Warsaw,
inv. no. M.Ob. 493

Provenance: Probably royal Saxon collection; King
Stanislaw August Poniatowski, last king of Poland,
Warsaw, 1795; Lazienski Palace, Warsaw (cat. 1931, no.
127); in the National Gallery, Warsaw, as of 1945;
Collecting Point, Munich 1947.

Exhibitions: Budapest, Szépmüvészeti Múzeum
(Museum of Fine Arts), *Holland Mestermürek a XVII.
Századból, A Varsói Nemzeti Múzeum és a Szépmüvészeti
Múzeum anyagábó*, 1967, no. 6; Lódz, Muzeum Sztuki,
*Arcydziela malarstwa holenderskiego XVII Wieku Ze zbiorów
polskich*, cat. by A. Chudzikowdki, 1967, no. 6;
Braunschweig, Herzog Anton Ulrich-Museum, Utrecht,
Centraal Museum, Cologne, Wallraf-Richartz Museum,
and Munich, Alte Pinakothek, *Europäische Malerei des
Barock aus dem Nationalmuseum Warschau*, 1989–90,
no. 38; Frankfurt 1993, no. 10.

Literature: F. de Piles, *Voyages de deux Français en
Allemagne, Danemark, Suéde, Russie et Pologne, fait en
1790–1792*, vol. 5 (Paris 1796), p. 44; A. Somov, *Katalog
kartin nachdjasèichsja v imperatorskom Lazenkovskom dvorce v
Varsar* (Warsaw, 1895), no. 147; L. Niemojeski, *Lazienki
Królewski oraz znajduj1ce siê w nich dzie3a sztuki* (Warsaw,
1923), no. 147; S. Iskierski, *Katalog Galerij obrazów w
Pa3acu w Lazienkach w Warszawie* (Warsaw, 1931), no.
127; T. Maňkowski, *Galerja Stanis3awa Augusta*, 2 vols.
(Lvov, 1932), no. 42, pl. 65; E. Plietzsch, *Gerard ter Borch*
(Vienna, 1944), p. 41; J. Bia3ostocki and M. Walicki,
*Europäische Malerei in polnischen Sammlungen
1300–1800* (Warsaw, 1957), fig. 313; Gudlaugsson
1959–60, vol. 1, p. 114, no. 129, ill. on p. 288, vol. 2, p.
143, no. 129; *Galeria Malarstwa Obcego, Przewodnik.
Muzeum Narodowe w Warszawie* (Warsaw, 1964), pp. 52-
53, 111, no. 23; *Malarstwo Europejskie*, 2 vols. (Warsaw,
1967), vol. 1, p. 123, no. 125, ill.; *Catalogue of Paintings,
Foreign Schools, National Museum in Warsaw*, 2 vols.
(Warsaw, 1969–70), no. 125; *Mezzotinta XVII–XVIII W.*,
Muzeum Narodowe (Breslau, 1971), no. 259; The
Hague/Münster 1974, p. 150; Sutton 1990, fig. 10-1;
Kettering 2000, p. 113.

Copies: Oil on canvas, 40.7 x 29.2 cm, with Feldmann,
Paris, 1929 (evaluated for him by Hofstede de Groot as a
copy). A weak, though probably contemporary work
(Gud.; photo RKD). A mantelpiece can just be discerned

in the background behind the soldier; and a copy,
Museum Bruckenthal in Sibiu (Romania).

Print: Johann Gottfried Haid (1710–1776), engraving,
1768, attributing it to Frans van Mieris.

Two figures lost in concentration enliven an
otherwise dark and undefined space, with a mantelpiece
vaguely indicated in the background. Perhaps this is a
drawing room, which would characterize the space as an
officer's billet. Seated in profile in a slat-backed chair at
the right is a young officer. Lips parted, he composes his
missive on a simple square wooden table: all that we see
is his hand holding the quill—a slender white arc at the
very center of the composition—and the top of the sheet
of paper behind his plumed hat resting to the front of
the tabletop. He wears a cuirass over a gold-ribbed
jerkin, beribboned breeches in this same material, and
stockings. Lying asleep at his foot just under the table is
a spaniel. Littering the ground at the left are bits of a
broken pipe and at the right the top half of a feather,
probably cut from the quill.

Observing him at the left is a *tambour-major*
(trumpeter). Standing casually, in profile to the right,
right arm akimbo and legs widespread, he awaits the
letter he will soon be charged with delivering. He sports
a red fur-trimmed hat embellished with gold and a
distinctive, dark blue tabard with black-and-gold stripes
and hanging sleeves made of a striped, gold-embroidered
fabric. Silver satinlike sleeves emerge from the
overgarment revealing a modest white linen cuff at the
wrist. He also wears a sword hung from a buff-colored
bandolier edged with gold embroidery. His trumpet
rests on his back, slung from a blue and gold cord. His
leggings are dark brown; his boots have spurs. Fashioned
from livery, this attractive attire was used consistently
by ter Borch. The trumpeter's clothes and certainly his
hat provide the only color accent in the otherwise
monochromatic palette.

This painting was traditionally thought to be the
companion to ter Borch's *An Officer Reading a Letter* in
the Gemäldegalerie, Dresden (cat. 6). They were together
in the royal Saxon collection in the eighteenth century.
The paintings have the same upright format, a similar
composition, a dark, undefined interior, and identical
table, chair, and figures, though in reverse. This view,
however, is no longer held. Writing on the painting in
the *Leselust* exhibition, Wercke notes that the courier's
garb deviated somewhat—for instance, the shirt of the
Warsaw trumpeter has no stripes—and that the figures
were not the same. The most notable difference is the
introduction of a third person behind and between the
reader and the courier. While probably not meant as

pendants, the Warsaw painting is close to the work in Dresden in its formal and thematic simplicity. Both seem a step removed from the more elegant depictions of accomplished pastimes of cultivated individuals presented in the other, slighter later related works, and indeed in many of ter Borch's genre themes. Yet neither are they fully in keeping with the "gallant officer" genre as portrayed earlier in the century by ter Borch, Willem Duyster, Pieter Codde, and others, with soldiers being the butt of ridicule and apprehension. The officers and trumpeters in Warsaw and Dresden are presented with dignity and respect for their office.

Gudlaugsson dated the Warsaw painting to about 1657–58, and it is probably the earliest of ter Borch's depictions of writing and reading in a soldier's milieu (Braunschweig et al. 1989–90, p. 136), the two closest works being *Officer Writing a Letter with a Trumpeter (The Dispatch)* (cat. 8) and *Officer Dictating a Letter while a Trumpeter Waits* (National Gallery, London). Compared with the Philadelphia picture, the Warsaw work exhibits stronger contrasts of light and dark, as well as a bolder use of color. The setting is far less elaborate in terms of both the number and quality of the objects and furnishings depicted. It lacks the elegance of a room with a canopy bed, carved mantelpiece, and table covered with a tablecloth. Moreover, here all the attention is focused on the epistolary activity, whereas the trumpeters in the London and Philadelphia works gaze out at the viewer, inviting participation. Finally, while the contents of the letters in the London and Philadelphia works are probably amorous in nature, as indicated by the ace of hearts on the ground in the Philadelphia picture and the fact that such a card was painted over (near the dog's foot) in the London one, no such indication is found in the Warsaw painting, leaving open the question of the kind of letter, or orders, being drafted. It is worth bearing in mind that at the time there was an unprecedented traffic of paper among civilians and military alike (D. Kunzle, *From Criminal to Courtier: The Soldier in Netherlandish Art, 1550–1672* [Leiden, 2002]).

Ter Borch addressed military themes throughout his life, but it became an important category within his oeuvre in the 1650s and 1660s after the conclusion of the Eighty Years' War. In fact, over one-third of his mature genre paintings include soldiers and officers. Rather than gaming, or carousing, the soldiers read or write letters— an activity almost exclusively associated with refined, elegant, educated ladies. Ter Borch's introduction of the military figure writing letters was a complete novelty and corresponds formally, thematically, and chronologically with the letter-writing woman. He painted three, all mentioned above, as well as two receiving letters, pictures now in The Hague and Dresden.

Although the trumpeter played a role in paintings by Codde, Jacob Ochtervelt, and others, he was an especially remarkable feature in ter Borch's works of this theme, one he portrayed no fewer than eight times in addition to the present painting. A symbolic pivot in the transition from military to civilian society, the trumpeter in fact fulfilled an actual military position, as Kettering has shown (2000). He served the cavalry, sounding the commander's orders and calling men awake. More highly paid than an ordinary soldier, the trumpeter also lodged with the officers. As a class they enjoyed diplomatic immunity and were normally not armed or armored, though they wore swords as gentlemen. Their real weapon was that "haughty aristocrat of musical instruments," the trumpet itself (D. Smithers, *The Music and History of the Baroque Trumpet before 1721* [Carbondale, Ill., 1988], p. 72). The associations generated by the trumpeter were positive, and his judiciousness, discretion, subtlety, and wit were emphasized in the seventeenth century, for instance in a military manual, Cruso's Militarie Instructions (n.d., p. 14). He was expected to look good, to be "of comely figure, good deportment . . . politick, discreet and cunning" (Elton, *Compleat Body of the Art Military*, 1650, cited in H. G. Farmer, *The Rise and Development of Military Music* [London, 1912], p. 40). In short, his office was that of a soldier-courtier, a peacemaker, bound to chivalrous codes; he had to negotiate the surrender of a town or, as in ter Borch's depictions, the surrender of a woman perhaps. His position in delicate matters is clear in the correspondence between Constantijn Huygens, the stadholder's secretary, from camp to the stadholder's wife, Amalia von Solms (Kunzle 2002, p. 611 n. 59).

Ter Borch's trumpeter, however, is not always the dignified fellow we have met above. While his bearing is such in the works in London, Philadelphia, Warsaw, Dresden, and The Hague, he joins in the carousing in the work in Paris and displays his amusement at delivering a letter to a sleeping soldier in the painting in Cincinnati (see Sutton essay).

–JK

GERARD TER BORCH
An Officer Writing a Letter with a Trumpeter, 1658–59
Signed lower right on the crosspiece: *GTBorch* (GTB in ligature)
Oil on canvas, 56.8 x 43.8 cm
Philadelphia Museum of Art: The William L. Elkins Collection, E1924-3-21

Provenance: (Possibly) sale, Petronella de la Court, widow of Adam Oortmans, Amsterdam, October 19, 1707, no. 31; Jan and Pieter Bisschop, Rotterdam, by 1752 (after Jan's death the collection sold as a whole to Adriaen and Jan Hope, Amsterdam); Henry Philip Hope, 1833; Henry Thomas Hor, 1854; Lord Francis Pelham Clinton Hope, London, cat. 1898, no. 70; the entire Hope Collection sold to dealer P. & D. Colnaghi and A. Wertheimer, London, 1898; W. L. Elkins, Philadelphia, cat. 1900, no. 129; acquired by the Philadelphia Museum of Art, 1924.

Exhibitions: Victoria and Albert Museum, London, 1891–98 (on loan from Lord Francis Pelham Clinton Hope); The Hague/Münster 1974, no. 41, ill.; Philadelphia/London/Berlin 1984, no. 10, pl. 69; Frankfurt 1993, no. 11, ill.

Literature: Smith, vol. 4 (1833), p. 121, no. 11; *The Hope Collection of Pictures of the Dutch and Flemish Schools* (London, 1898), no. 70, ill.; Hofstede de Groot, vol. 5 (1913), p. 16, no. 51; Gudlaugsson 1959–60, vol. 1, no. 143; Robinson 1974, p. 40; Sutton 1990, no. 10; Sutton n.d., pp. 1–10; Kettering 2000, pp. 110–15, fig. 2.

An officer sits at a table and composes a letter as a trumpeter who will act as messenger stands respectfully with hat in hand to the left. A slender white, spotted hound sniffs the courier. In the background is a pavilion bed, and on the right wall stands a tall hearth with breasted chimney with pilasters, wooden molding, *rabat* (cloth valance), and resting on the mantel above, a small vial of liquid and a powder horn. The officer wears a gold jacket with the sleeves decorated with narrow, horizontal bands, gray trousers, and a cuirass. He is placed, not in profile, but seated directly in front of the viewer at an oak table with red cloth cover. Before him is a piece of paper, tiny inkwell, writing utensils, and red sealing wax. The trumpeter wears a blue-and-black striped tabard over a light tan coat and white cravat and holds a tan hat. A long trumpet with tassel is slung over his shoulder by a yellow sash. The end of his long sword is just visible hanging down beneath the trumpet, suggesting the possibility of violence on his routes. The

sword casts a shadow in a room that is otherwise mostly illuminated by even daylight. The trumpeter, who glances out of the corner of his eye directly at the viewer, apparently waits for the officer to finish his letter. Completing the trumpeter's outfit are thigh-high, leather boots with spurs, indicating that he has arrived by horseback, hence capable of delivering express messages. On the wooden floor in the foreground are shards of a broken clay pipe and a single playing card, the ace of hearts.

Ter Borch had treated military themes since before he began his artistic career; a horseman drawn from the rear is ter Borch's earliest dated drawing (September 25, 1625), executed when he was only nine (Gudlaugsson 1959–60, vol. 1, p. 175, ill.). About 1640 he began to paint guardroom scenes in the tradition of Pieter Codde and Willem Duyster (q.v.), which depict officers and common footsoldiers gaming and relaxing in taverns, guardrooms, and sometimes camped in a disorderly fashion out-of-doors. Occasionally fights break out (Gudlaugsson, no. 26), but by and large these are idle gatherings of bored soldiers, whiling away their time, sometimes with lady companions, as they await marching orders. When the call to arms finally comes, it is delivered by the trumpeter who was the military's official messenger and courier; the earliest dated painting by ter Borch of a trumpeter is the so-called *Unwelcome News* dated 1653 (Sutton essay, *fig. 4*), in which he stands before the officer and his girlfriend in much the same attire and pose as in the present work. The trumpeter recurs in six other scenes by ter Borch (see Gudlaugsson 1959–60, nos. 121, 123, 124, 129, 130, and 141). While in some of these paintings he enters into the rowdy silliness of the tavern, sounding the call to drink up or tickling awake one of their own who has dozed off, in the paintings from Warsaw, Dresden, and London (see cats. 6 & 8, and cat. 8, *fig. 1*), he stands patiently to one side as the officer reads, writes, or dictates a letter. The settings of the present work and the London painting—which also features the tall hearth with columns, pavilion bed, and a covered table—also evoke a more respectably middle- or upper-class setting than the crude lodgings of the earlier soldier paintings. The fact that the officer composes in one and dictates a letter in the other also introduces a quieter, more reflective, and civilized note into the raucous guardroom tradition.

A conspicuous clue to the content of the officer's letter is the ace of hearts playing card that appears on the floor beside the dog's foot. In the painting in London (cat. 8, *fig.1*), another ace of hearts also appeared but was painted out by the artist, though it is still visible in the *repentir*; ter Borch may have edited it out because he felt it was too conspicuous a romantic sign, since the card

predates Netscher's departure from his master's studio in Deventer in 1658–59. This suggests that the present pair of paintings were the first pendants to link a man and a woman through the theme of a shared letter. Gabriel Metsu would later develop this idea to its greatest expression in his famous pendants in Dublin (cats. 18 & 19). The complementarity of these paintings emphasizes the ideal of the dialogue implicit in the letter theme and celebrates its capacity for romantic communication.

–PCS

Fig. 1. Gerard ter Borch
An Officer Dictating a Letter, c. 1655–58
Monogrammed
Oil on canvas, 74.5 x 51 cm
National Gallery, London, no. 5847

Fig. 2. Gerard ter Borch
The Letter Refused
Fully signed on the letter
Panel, 56 x 46.5 cm
Bayerische Staatsgemäldesammlungen, Alte Pinakothek, Munich, no. 206

makes it abundantly clear that the officer addresses the recipient "from the heart." We know that military messengers delivered private as well as official letters; ter Borch's painting in Munich (cat. 8, *fig. 2*) depicts a trumpeter trying to deliver a letter to an elegant and slyly smiling lady in her boudoir who appears to refuse it. In the present case we can be fairly certain that the officer's intended is the lady in the fur-trimmed jacket (cat. 9) that complements the present work in virtually all details—the mirroring of the standing and seated figures, the hearth, the covered bed and the same table, and the allied themes of a man writing a letter and a woman sealing her letter of response. Since the measurements of the latter work were long mistakenly recorded, the two paintings were not recognized as the same size and hence as probable companion pieces until the latter work resurfaced on the art market about five years ago (see Sutton n.d.). The model for the officer in the present work (as well as for the London painting) was probably ter Borch's pupil, Caspar Netscher. Therefore we can assume with considerable certainty that the painting

CASPAR NETSCHER

(Heidelberg or Prague c. 1636–1684 The Hague)

According to early sources (Houbraken, Weyerman), Caspar Netscher was born in Heidelberg (or possibly Prague) around 1636, the son of Johannes Netscher, a sculptor or engineer originally from Stuttgart, and Elizabeth Vetter, daughter of a Heidelberg Burgermeister. Nothing of this can be documented, however, and Caspar's parents might well have been the Amsterdam painter Johannes Nesscher or Netscher, and Susanna Jans., who married in Rotterdam in 1632. Early biographers tell of the death of Netscher's father in Germany and his mother's flight to the Netherlands through the strife and famine of the Thirty Years' War. Widow Netscher and her son eventually arrived in Arnhem, where Caspar received lessons in drawing from the Caravaggesque painter Hendrick Coster (1638–1659).

In about 1654–55 Netscher entered the Deventer studio of Gerard ter Borch. The date of his apprenticeship is substantiated in part by his signed copy of ter Borch's Paternal *Admonition*, dated 1655 (Schlossmuseum, Gotha) and by the inclusion of Netscher's distinctive saturnine features in several of ter Borch's guardroom and genre scenes of the mid-to-late 1650s (see cat. 8).

Netscher probably stayed four or five years in ter Borch's studio; then, determined to further his artistic education in Italy, set out on a ship bound for Bordeaux. He arrived in Bordeaux in early or mid-1659 and married Margareta Godijn, the daughter of a local mathematician, on November 25, 1659. The couple's first child, Theodoor, was born Bordeaux in 1661. Netscher and his family returned to the Netherlands the following year and settled in The Hague, where he resided for the rest of his life.

In October 1662 Netscher joined the Hague painters' confraternity Pictura and in 1668 joined the Witte Vendel company of the Sint Sebastiaansschutterij (St. Sebastian's militia guild). Twelve children were born to Netscher and his wife; of the nine who survived to adulthood at least two—Theodoor (1661–1728) and Constantijn (1668–1723)—became painters, and Johannes (1665–after 1715) became a jeweler and silversmith.

Caspar Netscher died in The Hague on January 15, 1684, his passing marked by several brief epitaphs written by the aged poet Constantijn Huygens. A detailed estate inventory made after Margareta Godijn's death in 1694 offers a measure of Netscher's financial success: in addition to a quantity of jewelry and household goods, the inventory lists 179 paintings, numerous books, portfolios, and other works of art.

Netscher began his career as a painter of genre scenes and portraits, very clearly indebted to the simple domestic interiors and politely reserved likenesses produced by Gerard ter Borch. By the mid-1660s Netscher had developed a more decorative style suitable to portraying the amusements and social ambitions of the wealthy elite. From about 1670 until his death, Netscher was primarily known as a painter of elegant (and enormously influential) small-scale portraits that expressed the cosmopolitan sophistication of a newly "aristocratized" Dutch patriciate. Netscher established a very productive atelier that continued to produce portraits in his manner well into the eighteenth century.

–MEW

Literature: Houbraken, vol. 1 (1718), pp. 92–96; Jakob Campo Weyerman, *De Leven-beschryvingen der Nederlandsche Konst-schilders en Konst-schilderessen* (Dordrecht, 1769), vol. 4, pp. 124–40; A. Bredius, "Een en ander over Caspar Netscher," *Oud Holland* 5 (1887), pp. 263–74; Pieter Marinus Netscher, *Heslachtsregister der Familie Netscher, met levensschetsen van de schilders Caspar, Theodorus, en Constantyn* (The Hague, 1889); Hofstede de Groot, vol. 5 (1913); exh. cat. Amsterdam 1989–90, pp. 155–80; Wieseman 2002.

Cat. 11.
CASPAR NETSCHER
Man Writing a Letter, 1664
Oil on panel, 27 x 18.5 cm
Signed and dated on map on rear wall: *CNetscher. fecit. 166[4?]* (C and N in ligature)
Gemäldegalerie Alte Meister, Staatliche Kunstsammlungen, Dresden, inv. 1346

Provenance: Acquired via Hofkommissar Raschke, possibly in Antwerp, for Augustus the Strong, Elector of Saxony, before 1722; mentioned in the Dresden inventory of 1722, no. A 518 ("Ein Gelehrter schreibt einen Brief").

Exhibitions: Moscow, Pushkin Museum, *Vystavka kartin Drezdenskoi gallerei: Katalog*, 1955; Berlin, National-Galerie, *Gemälde der Dresdner Galerie: vergeben von der Regierung der UdSSR an die Deutsche Demokratische Republik*, 1955–56; Dresden, *Gemäldegalerie, Ausstellung der Gemälde von der Regierung der UdSSR an die Deutsche Demokratische Republik vergebenen Meisterwerke*, 1956;

Amsterdam, Rijksmuseum, *De Hollandse Fijnschilders: van Gerard Dou tot Adriaen van der Werff*, cat. by Peter Hecht, 1989–90, no. 31.

Literature: Smith, vol. 4 (1833), no. 68 (as "Portrait of the Artist"; valued at 120 guineas); D. Franz Kugler, *Kandbook of Painting: The German, Flemish and Dutch Schools*, enl. and ed. G. F. Waagen, vol. 2 (London, 1860), p. 368 (dated 1664; possibly a self-portrait); Dresden, cat. 1856, p. 286, no. 1443 (possibly a self-portrait); Gustav F. C. Parthey, *Deutscher Bildersaal: Verzeichnis der in Deutschland vorhandenen Oelbilder verstorbener Maler aller Schulen*, vol. 2 (Berlin, 1864), p. 190 (as dated 1664; possibly a self-portrait); Carl Gustav Carus, *Betrachtungen und Gedanken für auserwählte Bilder der Dresdner Galerie* (Dresden, 1867), pp. 70f.; Dresden, cat. 1880, p. 371 (as dated 1665); Dresden, cat. 1908, p. 434 (notes 1722 inventory); Alfred Wurzbach, *Niederländisches Künstler-Lexikon*, vol. 2 (Vienna and Leipzig, 1910), p. 227 (possibly a self-portrait); Hofstede de Groot, vol. 5 (1913), no. 40; Plietzsch 1960, p. 61, fig. 91; S. J. Gudlaugsson, "Caspar Netscher," *Kindlers Malerei Lexikon*, vol. 4 (Zurich, 1967), p. 575, ill.; Robinson 1974, p. 93; exh. cat. Amsterdam 1989–90, pp. 156–59 (as dated 166[5?]); B. Werche, in Frankfurt 1993, p. 260; Wieseman 2002, pp. 57–58, 181, no. 23, colpl. 5.

Gazing pensively into space, a young man sits at a carpet-covered table with his chin resting heavily in his left hand. In his right hand he holds a quill pen poised above a blank sheet of paper; a silver inkwell set is close to hand. On the rear wall, suspended from metal rods, is a map of Prussia. The young man's fashionably understated dress—stylish blond curls and a billowing white chemise worn beneath a plain dark coat—echoes the sensitivity and elegant restraint of Netscher's composition.

Man Writing a Letter, one of Netscher's earliest ventures into the realm of high-life genre, deftly blends the simplicity of the artist's early depictions of domestic occupations and humble interiors with the elegant sophistication of later works chronicling the pastimes of the leisured class. The soft illumination, tonal palette, and smoky diffusion of the brushwork are a fitting manifestation of the dreamy abstraction of this young man, who is surely pondering the proper phrasing of a letter to his beloved. The map featured so prominently on the rear wall leads us to believe that he has traveled far from her side. Maps were traditionally associated with worldliness (see, among others, E. de Jongh, "Vermommingen van Vrouw Wereld in de 17de eeuw," in *Album Amicorum J. G. van Gelder*, ed. J. Bruyn et al. [The Hague, 1973], pp. 198–206), and the map of the Baltic region hung here is probably meant to connote

that the young man is somehow involved with the lively and lucrative trade that existed between the Netherlands and Baltic countries throughout the seventeenth century. The vast merchant fleet of the Northern Netherlands had long dominated the bulk-carrying trade in this area, exporting fish, meat, and dairy produce and importing grain and timber (see A. E. Christensen, *Dutch Trade in the Baltic about 1600* [Copenhagen, 1941], and J. A. Faber, "The Decline of the Baltic Grain-trade in the Second Half of the 17th Century," *Acta Historiae Neerlandica* 1 [1966]). Despite the map's implications, however, the absence of a secretary in this scene would tend to confirm that the man is attending to private rather than official correspondence.

Beneath his veneer of worldliness, the young man appears almost despondent, immobilized by the blank page before him; his pose, leaning his head into his hand, is a classic attribute of Melancholy (see cat. 22). The realization that the words he inscribes will be his sole emissary to a distant reader, coupled with the truly bewildering array of options offered up by contemporary letter-writing manuals for every occasion (see Sutton essay), could easily make penning a delicately nuanced missive conveying precisely the right balance of respect, admiration, and intent a daunting enterprise.

In composing this deceptively simple work Netscher appropriated elements of Gerard ter Borch's depictions of thoughtful female letter writers and readers: the deliciously evocative *Woman Writing a Letter* in the Mauritshuis (cat. 5) is particularly close to the present picture in conception and mood. Johannes Vermeer's *Woman Writing a Letter* (cat. 38) shares the tranquillity and formal restraint of Netscher's composition, although the young woman's outward gaze, pointedly engaging the viewer's complicity, creates a more dynamic narrative exchange. Comparable genre images of solitary men writing letters are rare, however. Portraits of scholars or officials writing letters—some assisted by their secretary or amanuensis—abound, and ter Borch and others painted genre scenes of officers composing letters with a uniformed *trompeter* standing by, and with or without male companions eager to offer guidance and advice. Netscher certainly knew these latter compositions, as he had posed for at least two of them during his apprenticeship in ter Borch's studio during the late 1650s: *Officer Writing a Letter (The Dispatch)* (Philadelphia Museum of Art, cat. 8) and *Officer Dictating a Letter* (cat. 8, *fig. 1*). Yet he chose to depict a more contemplative, less proactive aspect of the letter-writing process, crafting a subtle internal exploration of the mental and emotional effort that inevitably preceded setting pen to paper, rather than exploring the narrative possibilities created by introducing other figures into the composition.

Gabriel Metsu's painting of a man writing a letter, in the National Gallery of Ireland (c. 1662–65; cat. 18), offers perhaps the closest comparison to Netscher's solitary scribe. When considered with its pendant of a woman reading a letter (cat. 19), however, this painting becomes one component in an external dialogue rather than a completely self-contained image. Metsu's letter writer is, moreover, more directed in his task and shares little of the wistful melancholy so appealing in Netscher's painting. One might also consider a relationship between Netscher's *Man Writing a Letter* and depictions of melancholic students and scholars in their studies; compare, for example, Michiel Sweerts's *Portrait of a Young Man*, dated 1656 (Hermitage, St. Petersburg,), or Jan Davidsz. de Heem's *Interior with a Man Seated at a Table*, dated 1628 (Ashmolean Museum, Oxford).

Netscher's inscribed *ricordo* drawing of *Man Writing a Letter*, retained in the studio when the painting itself was sold, is in the British Museum (brush and ink, 152 x 122 mm, inv. 1895-9-15-1227; see Wieseman 2002, pp. 115, 181, fig. 58).

—MEW

Cat. 12.
CASPAR NETSCHER
The Letter with the Black Seal, 1665
Signed and dated upper right: *CNetscher Fecit 1665.* (C and N in ligature)
Oil on panel, 30.9 x 26.5 cm
Staatliches Museum, Schwerin, inv. G 2347

Provenance: Probably collection Adriaen Bout (d. 1733), The Hague; acquired for the duke of Mecklenburg between 1725 and 1791, probably in the sale, Adriaen Bout, The Hague, August 11, 1733, no. 62 ("een Nagt-ligje,Verbeeldende een Juffer en een Meyd, die aan haar een Brief overgeeft, 12 x 10 1/2 duim," f 205 to van Haften [agent for Christian Ludwig II von Mecklenburg]); removed to Paris, Musée du Louvre, by Napoleon's troops, 1807–15; Schloss, Ludwigslust (1821); thence to the museum.

Exhibitions: Yokohama, Sogo Museum of Art, *Niederländische Malerei und Grafik des 17. Jahrhunderts aus dem Staatlichen Museum Schwerin*, 1988, no. 40; Frankfurt 1993, no. 61, ill.

Literature: Possibly Gerard Hoet, *Catalogus of Naamlyst van schilderyen* (The Hague, 1752), vol. 1, p. 389 (Bout sale); Jakob Campo Weyerman, *De Leven-beschryvingen der Nederlandsche Konst-schilders en Konst-schilderessen* (Dordrecht, 1769), vol. 4, p. 134 (as in Bout collection, "een Nachtlicht, verbeeldende een jonge Juffer, welke een Brief overgeeft aan haar Kamenier"); Johann Gottfried Groth, *Verzeichnis der Gemälde in der Herzoglichen Gallerie* (Schwerin, 1792), p. 18, no. EI 22; Schwerin/Ludwigslust, cat. 1821, no. 145; Smith, vol. 4 (1833), no. 40, Smith, *Supplement* (1842), no. 28; Hofstede de Groot, vol. 5 (1913), no. 133; Schwerin, cat. 1962, no. 274; Schwerin, cat. 1982, p. 111; B. Werche, in Frankfurt 1993, pp. 258–59; Wieseman 2002, pp. 159, 190–91, no. 36, pl. 36.

Engraved: François Dequevauvillers, as *La Mauvaise Nouvelle*, in Musée Français.

In a darkened interior lit by a single candle, a woman reacts with surprise and dismay to the letter being shown to her by a maidservant standing in the shadows. The seated woman is elegantly dressed in a white satin skirt and a dark red velvet dressing jacket trimmed with fur; her hands are raised in an elegantly spontaneous gesture of distress. Her companion, more soberly dressed, holds a handkerchief to her eyes as she tenders the letter with its ominous black seal. On the table is a shallow silver basin with its lid partially removed, from which trails a red ribbon.

There seems little doubt that the tearful maid is delivering news of a death. The use of black sealing wax, so plainly visible here, was reserved for letters containing notifications of death or letters of mourning and condolence. Immediately following a death, couriers were dispatched to friends and relatives of the deceased, bearing verbal announcements, printed notifications, or handwritten letters with the sorrowful news and an invitation to the funeral. Seventeenth-century diarists note all too frequently the sending and receiving of these missives, reflecting the era's high mortality rates. Extant letters relating news of a death (as well as published exemplars) often contained copiously detailed descriptions of the deceased's final hours, affording the recipient at least a vicarious presence at the deathbed. At the other end of the epistolary spectrum, Jean Puget de la Serre's popular letter-writing manual includes a poignantly brief "Letter from a Widdow, certifying a friend of her Husband's death": "Sir, This Sorrowful Letter shall inculcate nothing but death into your memorie, assuring you that you have lost a most real admirer, and faithful servant, in the Person of my Husband. Pardon me if I say no more; the Pen fals out of my hand, and my tears blot out my writing: I am the most afflicted Woman in the World" (Puget de la Serre 1640, p. 102). Netscher's use of a single candle to light the scene—its flame struggling ineffectually against the encroaching shadows—enhances the pathetic impact of the letter.

The gleaming silver basin on the table adds a poignant detail to the sad drama unfolding in Netscher's painting. The basin's lid has been partially removed, and a red ribbon is draped over the side. A similar motif— an earthenware brazier filled with coals, with a ribbon dangling from it—is included in several of Jan Steen's paintings of despondent and lovesick maidens. A brazier is prominently situated (together with a discarded letter) in the foreground of Steen's *Doctor's Visit* in the Philadelphia Museum of Art (see cat. 32, *fig. 2*); others are visible in Steen's versions of the theme in the Rijksmuseum, Amsterdam; Mauritshuis, The Hague; Taft Museum, Cincinnati; and Wellington Museum, London, among others. This unusual detail has frequently been interpreted as a sly indicator of seventeenth-century medical quackery: it was purportedly a method employed by charlatans to detect pregnancy, based on the smell produced by burning a ribbon from the afflicted woman's garments. However, burnt ribbon seems actually to have been used as a restorative—a primitive form of smelling salts—for reviving fainting women to consciousness. (On the motif and its various interpretations, see P. C. Sutton, Jan Steen: *Comedy and Admonition, Philadelphia Museum of Art Bulletin* 78 [winter 1982–spring 1983], pp. 21–24, and L. S. Dixon, *Perilous Chastity* [Ithaca, 1995], pp. 143–47, both with further references.) The silver basin in Netscher's painting is rather more elegant than Steen's earthenware brazier, yet it surely served the same purpose: to revive the woman from a faint, in this instance brought on by the receipt of the letter with its unmistakably ominous seal.

This painting is mentioned in the 1735 inventory of the estate of the renowned Hague collector Adriaen Bout (d. April 16, 1733): "een dito [stuk door Casparus Netscher de Oude] Nagtligtje, verbeeldende een Juffe en een Meyd die aen haer een brieff overgeeft" (a night scene by Caspar Netscher, depicting a young lady and a maid who gives her a letter; see Wieseman 2002, p. 159, doc. 161 [dated November 3, 1735], no. 62). An old copy after this painting, attributed to Godfried Schalcken, is in the Suermondt-Ludwig-Museum, Aachen (oil on panel, 37 x 30 cm; inv. 462).

–MEW

Cat. 13. (Exhibited in Dublin only)
CASPAR NETSCHER
Young Woman with a Letter and a Medallion, 1667
Signed and dated upper right: *CNetscher. fe. 1667* (C and
N in ligature)
Oil on panel, 26 x 21.5 cm
Gemäldegalerie Alte Meister, Staatliche Museen, Kassel,
inv. GK 291

Provenance: In principal Kassel inventory of 1749;
removed to Paris (Louvre) by Napoleon's troops,
1807–15; returned 1815.

Exhibition: Frankfurt 1993, no. 62

Literature: Kassel, cat. 1783, pp. 62–63, no. 90; Smith,
Supplement (1842), no. 31; G. K. Nagler, *Neues allgemeines
Künstler-Lexikon*, vol. 11 (1840), p. 287 (as *Le portrait
chéri*); Gustav F. C. Parthey, *Deutscher Bildersaal: Verzeichnis
der in Deutschland vorhandenen Oelbilder verstorbener Maler
aller Schulen*, vol. 2 (Berlin, 1864), p. 189; Alfred
Wurzbach, *Niederländisches Künstler-Lexikon*, vol. 2
(Vienna and Leipzig, 1910), p. 227; Hofstede de Groot,
vol. 5 (1913), no. 131; Naumann 1981, vol. 1, p. 112 n.
147; Ydema 1991, p. 148 (depicts Transylvanian carpet);
B. Werche, in exh. cat. Frankfurt 1993, p. 260; A. Adams,
in ibid., p. 92; Kassel, cat. 1996, vol. 1, p. 204; Wieseman
2002, pp. 68–69, 115, 211–12, cat. 60, pl. 60.

A young woman sits at a table, holding an open
letter in her lap; in her right hand she holds a miniature
portrait of a man. A young boy, possibly the messenger
who has brought this missive with its welcome enclosure,
stands in the shadows at right. The woman's red satin
skirt is drawn up to reveal a white underskirt; her tight
bodice and decoratively slashed sleeves exude voluptuous
billows of a white chemise. Carefully curled and plaited,
her blond hair is adorned with a thin red ribbon and a
strand of pearls. A swath of curtain draped across the
top of the image extends down the left side to form a
dark repoussoir against the light emanating from the left.
On the carpet-covered table are a round silver box and
a mirror. The painting on the rear wall appears to be a
floral still life, with an elaborately carved and gilded
frame.

The young woman smiles—even a bit smugly—as she
proudly brandishes the portrait miniature. Although we
cannot be certain, it seems most likely that the miniature
has arrived together with letter she holds in her lap. The
presentation of a miniature portrait by a suitor to his
lover occurs earlier in Netscher's oeuvre, in *Presentation
of a Medallion Portrait* of about 1658–60 *(fig. 1)*. In that
scene, a messenger (or perhaps the suitor himself) kneels

Cat. 16

Cat. 16.
GABRIEL METSU
Man Writing a Letter
Signed on the book: *G Metsu*
Oil on panel, 25 x 24 cm
Musée Fabre, Montpellier, inv. 836.4.38

Provenance: Sale, the Dowager Boreel, Amsterdam, September 23, 1814, no. 9 (2,205 fl. to van Spaan); sale, Stanley's, London, 1815 (bought in); sale, Madame Le Rouge, Paris, April 27, 1818 (2,450 francs); sale, Lapeyrière, Paris, April 19, 1825 (10,110 francs); acquired by Valedau of Paris, before 1833 (10,000 francs); bequeathed to the Musée Fabre, Montpellier, cat. 1890, no. 715.

Exhibition: Frankfurt 1993, no. 55.

Literature: Smith, vol. 1 (1833), no. 69; Hofstede de Groot, vol. (1907), no. 24; Plietzsch 1936, pp. 1, 5, ill.; Gudlaugsson 1968, pp. 29, 34 n. 72; Robinson 1974, pp. 39–41, pl. 75; Robinson 1985, n.p., fig. 2; Moiso-Diekamp 1987, pp. 367–68, no. B 1; Broos, in The Hague/ San Francisco 1990–91, p. 330, fig. 1; Ydema 1991, p. 138, no. 126; Sutton n.d., p. 11 n. 29.

A man seated at a table has paused momentarily as he writes a letter, holding his quill pen above the paper. He has long curly hair and a mustache and wears a brown coat with silver trim and gray britches. The heavy oak table is covered with an oriental carpet (identified by Ydema as a Lotto carpet). On it rest a silver inkstand, a second feather pen, and a small book with a marker in the pages. At the back left is a bookcase covered with a cloth and surmounted with a ceramic jug, paper and folders, a box, and a document with a red seal. A woman approaches from the shadows bringing a lighted candle.

This painting appeared in sales in 1814, 1815, and 1818 with a pendant, *Young Woman Receiving Letter*, now in the Timken Museum of Art (cat.17). It is likely that Metsu conceived these works as companion pieces. Not only are they the same size, but they have cleverly complementary three-quarter-length designs. In the present work the man is turned to the right working by the fading light of day as a woman brings a candle. In the San Diego painting, the woman is turned to the left, seated in sunshine beneath an airy portico with a view to a Palladian villa as a young man delivers her the message. Before her is a stone table that is aligned with that of the man when the two paintings are hung side by side. With their hands both slightly raised, he in midthought and she to receive the letter, even their gestures seem reciprocal.

Several writers have observed that the main figures in these two paintings may actually portray the artist and his wife. Gabriel Metsu was married to Isabella de Wolff on April 12, 1658. The figures' likenesses are known from several portraits, including the pendants in the Speed Museum, Louisville (*figs. 1 & 2*). The resemblance to the writer's long nose, full face, receding hairline, and long curly hair is notable.

The present pair of paintings are usually dated to the late 1650s (Robinson) or about 1660 (Gudlaugsson), when Metsu moved from Leiden to Amsterdam and began to reveal his indebtedness to Dou and the *fijnschilders* in both style and subject matter. The mastery

Fig. 1. Gabriel Metsu
Self-Portrait
Oil on panel, 20 x 16 cm
Gift of the Museum Collectors,
Collection of The Speed Art Museum,
Louisville, Kentucky, no. 1970.56.1

Fig. 2. Gabriel Metsu
Portrait of the Artist's Wife, Isabella de Wolff
Oil on panel, 20 x 16 cm
Gift of the Museum Collectors,
Collection of The Speed Art Museum,
Louisville, Kentucky, no. 1970.56.2

of artificial illumination, either a candle or a lamp, was a specialty of Dou's, who painted several nocturnal scenes on a small scale with great detail. Metsu never aspired to the hard finish of Dou and always retained a more liquid touch and warmer palette, which won him many admirers. John Smith wrote in 1833 of these two paintings: "These pictures are painted with a broad and melting tenderness of colour, and are in every respect fine examples of the master." The idea of pairing the male letter writer with a female recipient in the companion piece was probably invented by ter Borch (see cats. 8 & 9). The arrangement serves to emphasize the reciprocity inherent in correspondence, a dialogue that was stressed as fundamental to good letter writing in the letter-writing manuals.

–PCS

Cat. 17.
GABRIEL METSU
A Young Woman Receiving a Letter, c. 1658
Signed lower left: *G. Metsu*
Oil on panel, 25.7 x 24.4 cm
The Putnam Foundation, Timken Museum of Art, San Diego, inv. no. 1958.01

Provenance: Sale, the Dowager Boreel, Amsterdam, September 23, 1814, no. 8 (950 fl. to van Yperen [*sic*]); with dealer van Iperen, Amsterdam, 1814; possibly King of Sardinia (see Broos, in The Hague/San Francisco 1990–91); sale, Stanley's, London, 1815 (bought in); sale, Madame Le Rouge, Paris, 1818 (5,080 francs, to Le Rouge); with dealer Nieuwenhuys, Brussels; collection August-Marie-Raimond, Prince of Arenberg, Brussels, before 1829; collection Duke of Arenberg, Brussels; with dealer Wildenstein & Co., New York, by 1958; acquired by the Putnam Trust for the Timken Art Gallery, San Diego, 1958.

Exhibition: The Hague/San Francisco 1990–91, no. 42, ill.

Literature: Smith, vol. 1 (1833), no. 70; Hofstede de Groot, vol. 1 (1907), no. 183; Plietzsch 1936, p. 5, fig.; Robinson 1974, pp. 39–41, 60, 81, fig. 76, ill. frontispiece and cover; Naumann 1981, p. 115–16; Robinson 1985, n.p., fig. 3; Moiso-Diekamp 1987, pp. 367–68, no. B1; exh. cat. Frankfurt 1993, p. 244, fig. 55.2; Sutton n.d., p. 11 n. 29.

A young woman in a gray-green skirt, red jacket, and white collar and hood sits with an open book on her lap

before a stone table. A servant boy dressed in a rusty brown coat and trousers doffs his hat deferentially and delivers a letter to the lady, who seems to have interrupted her reading. The suggestion of a smile crosses her lips. On the letter one can just make out the address, "Juffr[ouw] . . . ," indicating that the young woman is unmarried. On the table to the left is a stone urn with a prominent red poppy and other flowers. The suggestion of an elegant garden setting is introduced by the arches of an open arcade at the back and a glimpse of a grand Palladian villa in the distance. An even, soft daylight suffuses the scene and brings out the strong colors of the subtly harmonized palette.

This painting in all likelihood is the pendant to the painting by Metsu from Montpellier (cat. 16), which depicts a man writing a letter at a desk. The two paintings share early provenance, nearly identical dimensions, and complementary designs (see the commentary to the pendant, cat. 16). It also seems likely that the models for the letter writer and the pretty young woman depicted here were Metsu and his new bride, Isabella de Wolff. The portrait of Isabella in Louisville (see cat. 16, *fig. 2*), depicts a thoughtful young woman who closely resembles the lady depicted here. Her pert nose, high forehead, and set smile are similar in appearance. If we assume that the two primary figures in the scene are Metsu and Isabella, and that the latter was still a maid (*Juffrouw*), it is conceivable that the pair were painted just before their marriage on April 12, 1658—a date consistent with the style of the picture.

Notwithstanding questions of dating, this charming pair of pictures undoubtedly were inspired by ter Borch's companion pieces but refined the latter's concept of pendant paintings depicting a man and woman corresponding by letter. Here the young unmarried woman seems to have just received the letter sent by the man. By facing one another, the three-quarter-length designs also underscore their dialogue and communication. Naumann (1981, p. 116) suggested that the mansion in the background of the scene of the young woman could recall King David's palace and hence prompt associations with the Bathsheba story, and the book in her lap could recall Marian (virginal) imagery of a woman alone reading a book. Thus he suggested that the woman could be presented with the dilemma of temptation by the letter. Metsu returned to the challenge of pendants on the letter theme triumphantly about five to seven years later in his masterpiece pendants in Dublin (cats. 18 & 19).

–PCS

GABRIEL METSU
Man Writing a Letter, c. 1665–67
Signed upper right: *G. Metsu*
Oil on panel, 52.5 x 40.2 cm
National Gallery of Ireland, Dublin, Cat. no. 4536

Provenance: Sale, Hendrick Sorgh, Amsterdam, March 28, 1720, no. 29 (560 fl. with its pendant); sale, G. Bruyn, Amsterdam, March 16, 1724 (785 fl. with its pendant); Johannes Coop; Gerrit Braamcamp, Amsterdam, c. 1744–50; sale, G. Braamcamp, Amsterdam, July 31, 1771, no. 125 (5205 fl., with its pendant, to Jan Hope); Jan Hope; Lord Francis Pelham Clinton Hope, Deepdene, thence by descent; the collection purchased en bloc by A. Wertheimer and P. & D. Colnaghi, 1898; Sir Alfred Beit, London and Blessington; stolen in 1974 and 1986, but recovered in 1993; gifted by Sir Alfred Beit to the National Gallery of Ireland, 1987.

Exhibitions: London, British Gallery, 1815; London, Royal Academy of Arts, Winter Exhibition, 1881, no. 124, and 1900, no. 37; London, Burlington Fine Arts Club, 1900, no. 46; Leiden 1966, no. 23; Amsterdam 1976, no. 39; Amsterdam 2000, no. 141a, ill.

Literature: Smith, vol. 4 (1833), p. 80, no. 20; Waagen 1854, vol. 2, p. 116; Hofstede de Groot, vol. 1 (1907), pp. 311–12, no. 185; Bille 1961, p. 72; Robinson 1974, pp. 40, 59–61, 93, 97, pl. 145; Moiso-Diekamp 1987, pp. 100, 365–66, no. A 1; J. Bruyn, in exh. cat. Amsterdam/ Boston/Philadelphia 1987-88, pp. 92–93, fig. 14; Potterton et al. 1988, no. 5; Ydema 1991, p.164, no. 514; Wieseman 2002, pp. 58, 60, fig. 13.

A gentleman elegantly attired in black silk and ample white linen collar and sleeves sits with his ankles crossed writing a letter at a table with a quill pen. His beribboned black hat hangs on the back of the red upholstered chair. Before him on the table are a silver inkwell and a wafer stamp. The table is covered with a sumptuous Persian carpet with a red field and blue border with fringe. The leaded glass window in the left wall is open to admit the air and clear, silver light. Seen through the open window and resting on the table is a globe. On the whitewashed wall is a pastoral Italianate landscape with sheep and goats in the style of the followers of Adriaen van de Velde in a lovely carved and gilt frame with lobed decorations and surmounted by a dove. Birds also figure on the line of blue and white tiles at the base of the wall. The floor is composed of black and white marble in diamond patterns.

John Smith, who in 1833 (vol. 4, p. 71) commended

Metsu's "genius and taste," was probably referring to the present pair of paintings (cats. 8 & 9) when he noted that "some interest must be awakened by the inditing of an epistle;—the reception of its answer." Throughout their recorded history these two paintings have always appeared together as a pair, being sold and exhibited together. Depicting a man writing a letter and a woman reading a letter, they create a pictorial dialogue that underscores the reciprocal nature of the letter theme. The notion of companion pieces, one depicting a man writing a letter and the other, a woman reading it, was probably first introduced by Gerard ter Borch (see cats. 8 & 9); Metsu had probably treated this subject earlier in his companion paintings in Montpellier and San Diego (cats. 16 & 17). Whereas in the latter pair, the sender and recipient face each other in half-length compositions, here the designs are subtler, with the man turning his back to the woman as he concentrates on his writing while she leans toward him and the light. Cornelia Moiso-Diekamp's suggestion (1987) that the relationship of the two paintings should be reversed, with the woman's painting appearing on the left and the man's on the right, seems unlikely, as is her assumption that the second letter held by the maid is the letter written by the man. (She fails to note that it is addressed to Metsu.)

When the paintings were in the famous eighteenth-century collection of Gerrit Bramcamp in Amsterdam, Jean François de Bastide described them in *Le Temple des Arts, ou le Cabinet de Monsieur Braamcamp* (1766) and assumed that the young man was a student in his room writing to his mistress ("jeune Etudiant dans sa chamber . . . Il écrit une letter à sa maîtresse, comme il paroît par le pendant"). While the globe would suggest a man of learning, and together with his elegant furnishings and costume surely indicate a worldly person, even well-to-do students usually were depicted with books. However, it seems safe to assume that the missive that he sets to with such ardent concentration is directed to the young woman, who appears subtly gratified by what she reads. His more sumptuous surroundings, with the imported rug, marble floor, and fashionable Italianate landscape in ornate frame suggest the male sphere of public display, while the woman's room, though scarcely abstemious, stresses her more delimited world of domestic preoccupations. According to Onno Ydema, who has made a study of carpets represented in seventeenth-century Dutch paintings, Metsu depicted similar Persian as well as Lotto carpets in other genre scenes (compare cat.16). The actual frame that encircles the pastoral scene in the background is owned by Otto Naumann, New York.

—PCS

Cat. 19.
GABRIEL METSU
Woman Reading a Letter with a Maidservant, c 1665-67
Signed on the letter in the maid's hand: "Metsu tot
Amst [.....] port"
Oil on panel, 52.5 x 40.2 cm
National Gallery of Ireland, Dublin, Cat. no. 4537

Provenance: Sale, Hendrick Sorgh, Amsterdam, March
28, 1720, no. 29 (560 fl. with its pendant); sale, G. Bruyn,
Amsterdam, March 16, 1724 (785 fl. with its pendant);
Johannes Coop; Gerrit Braamcamp c. 1744–50; sale, G.
Braamcamp, Amsterdam, July 31, 1771, no. 125 (5205 fl.,
with its pendant, to Jan Hope); Jan Hope; Lord Francis
Pelham Clinton Hope, Deepdene, thence by descent; the
collection purchased en bloc by A. Wertheimer and P. &
D. Colnaghi, 1898; Sir Alfred Beit, London and
Blessington; stolen in 1974 and 1986, but recovered in
1993; gifted by Sir Alfred Beit to the National Gallery
of Ireland, 1987.

Exhibitions: London, British Gallery, 1815; London,
Royal Academy of Arts, Winter Exhibition, 1881, no.
125, and 1900, no. 38; London, Burlington Fine Arts
Club, 1900, no. 46; Leiden 1966, no. 23; Amsterdam
1976, no. 39; Amsterdam, Rijksmuseum, The Glory of
the Golden Age, April 15–September 17, 2000, no. 141b,
ill. and detail on the cover.

Literature: Smith, vol. 4 (London, 1833), p. 81, no. 21;
Waagen, 1854, vol. 2, p. 116; Hofstede de Groot, vol. 1
(1907), p. 311, no. 184; Robinson 1974, pp. 40, 59–61,
62, 85, 97, 191, pl. 146; Moiso-Diekamp 1987, pp.
365–66, no. A 1; J. Bruyn, in exh. cat. Amsterdam/
Boston/Philadelphia 1987-88, pp. 92-93, fig. 15;
Potterton et al. 1988, no. 6; Wieseman 2002, pp. 58, 60,
fig. 14.

A young woman sits on a little platform called a
soldertje as she reads a letter. Wearing a white cap, elegant
yellow fur-trimmed jacket, and peach silk skirt, she
evidently has interrupted her needlework; a lovely blue
and red sewing pillow rests in her lap, a sewing basket
appears at her side, and on the tile floor in the lower
right is an errant thimble. She inclines her head toward
the light provided by a window with a blue curtain on
the left and has kicked off a slipper that appears in the
foreground, probably to place her bare foot on the foot
warmer that resides unseen under her skirt. At the back
right a maidservant in more drab attire and apron stands
with her back to the viewer and rests a marketing pail
casually on her hip as she raises a bright green curtain
covering a painting of a seascape in a simple black frame.

Cat. 19, detail

In her left hand she holds a letter addressed to the artist, hence not, as has sometimes been assumed the envelope in which the letter came that the lady reads. A small mirror, in another black frame and surmounted with a ribbon, also appears on the whitewashed back wall. A small lapdog rests its front paws on the platform and looks up at the maidservant.

This pair of pendants are generally regarded not only as two of Metsu's greatest works but among the finest Dutch genre paintings ever produced. John Smith (1833) stated, "These productions are of the rarest excellence and beauty," and commended in the present work the "the singularly clear and luminous effect [that] pervades this picture." When exhibited recently at the Rijksmuseum they were described as "two masterpieces of the Golden Age." Franklin Robinson correctly characterized these pictures as late works by Metsu from his final years in Amsterdam, stressing the present work's debt to the lightened tonality, silvery light, and spatial clarity of the Delft School, notably in the works of Johannes Vermeer and Pieter de Hooch (q.q.v.). Earlier in Metsu's career, he had been more influenced by the refined and darker manner of the Leiden School painters that he had known in his youth.

As in his pendants in San Diego and Montpellier (see cats.16 & 17), the companionship of the two paintings here is subtly reinforced not only by the related subjects and the implication of a continuous narrative to be read from left to right but also by the compositions. Both depict the corner of a room with a window at the left through which an angled light descends, and each design is composed of a series of clear, rectangular forms. While the relative spareness and order of the present interior seems at first glance more restrained than the man's interior (Robinson speaks of the work's "sober frugality"), the lady's costly fabrics, the large curtained painting in what is probably an expensive ebony frame, the delicately wrought chair at the right, not to mention the maidservant and lapdog, indicate that this is a well-to-do household. As in earlier works by Dirck Hals (see cat. 2), Vermeer (fig.58; *The Love Letter*), and others, the painting of the seascape on the back wall may allude symbolically to the fact that her male correspondent is separated from her by a sea voyage. The seascape is also a scene of choppy seas; indeed, the authors of the Rijksmuseum's catalogue saw them as "tempestuous" and suggested that they alluded to the idea that "love is as fickle as the sea." However, unlike in Jan Steen's moralizing genre scenes on the theme of Easy Come, Easy Go (see, for example, the painting in the Boijmans-Van Beuningen Museum, Rotterdam, no. 2527), there is no figure of Fortuna (Fortune) here to augment the rough seascape's potential allusion to the unpredictable

nature of fortune and love.

Like de Hooch and other Dutch genre painters, Metsu was a keen observer of canines, favoring the papillon breed as a pet in his depictions of highborn ladies, and often juxtaposing different breeds of dogs that seemed appropriate to the sexes; note, for example, the evocative confrontation between the spaniel and the lapdog in Metsu's so-called *Hunter's Gift* (Rijksmuseum, Amsterdam, no. C 177).

–PCS

Cat. 20.
GABRIEL METSU
Woman Writing a Letter, c. 1665
Signed: *G Metsu*
Oil on panel, 39.4 x 33. 2 cm
Private Collection

Provenance: Sale, Dr. van Cleef, Hôtel Drouot, Paris, April 4, 1864, no. 59 (5020 francs); Marquis da Fosse, Lisbon; Charles T. Yerkes, New York; sale, Yerkes, American Art Association, New York, April 5–8, 1910, no. 98 ($17,000 to Kleinberger); Oscar Huldschinsky, Berlin; Simon James; sale, L. van den Bergh, Mak van Waay, Amsterdam, November 5, 1935, no. 13; acquired by Arthur Hartog of The Hague in Amsterdam, c. 1935, sold by his descendants; sale, Christie's, New York, January 27, 2000, no. 76, ill.

Exhibition: The Hague, Gemeentemuseum, *Oude Kunst uit Haagsche Bezit*, December 1936–February 1937, no. 100 (lent by Arthur Hartog).

Literature: *Magazine of Art*, March 1895; *A Catalogue of Paintings and Sculpture in the Collection of Charles T. Yerkes, Esq.*, vol. 1 (New York, 1904), no. 60, ill.; Hofstede de Groot, vol. 1 (1907), pp. 275–76, no. 76a; Robinson 1974, p. 85 n. 103 and p. 216, fig. 208; Ydema 1991, p. 164, no. 518 (with incorrect measurements).

An elegantly dressed woman viewed three-quarter-length sits writing a letter at a table covered with an oriental carpet and turns to smile at the viewer. She wears a black jacket trimmed with white fur, a mustard yellow skirt with vertical black stripes in the front, a white cowl and black skullcap, long earrings and pinkie ring. Delicately holding a quill pen, her hand is poised above a silver inkwell and a sheet of paper. At the lower right her lapdog, sporting a belled collar secured by a blue ribbon, strains toward her, standing on a red stool or box. In the shadows at the back right appears a seascape

Fig. 1. Gabriel Metsu
A Visit to the Nursery
Signed and dated: *1661*
Oil on canvas, 77.5 x 81.3 cm
The Metropolitan Museum of Art, New York, Gift of J.
Pierpont Morgan, 1917 (17.190.20)

in a gold frame covered with a blue-green curtain; and at the left is a large marble hearth.

The suggestion of a lighter-colored carved frieze and capital on the hearth suggests that it was inspired by the mantelpiece carved by Artus Quellinus for the Oude Raadzaal in the new Amsterdam Town Hall by Jacob van Campen. Metsu was an admirer of this fireplace, using it as a model for the mantelpiece in his well-known *Visit to the Nursery* in the Metropolitan Museum of Art, New York (*fig. 1*). Pieter de Hooch also employed details from the interior of the Town Hall to suggest ever grander private spaces in his genre scenes (see exh. cat. Amsterdam, Royal Palace, *The Royal Palace of Amsterdam in Paintings of the Golden Age*, 1997, pp. 22–27, 68–77). The use of curtains like the one that serves to protect the painting in the background was a common practice of the day (see cat.19). And similar Persian carpets with a red field, blue border, and fringe appear elsewhere in Metsu's art (see cat. 18) and hence seem to have been a favored prop. However, the fireplace confirms that the space here is fictional, like so many of the spaces depicted in high-life genre scenes from Dirck Hals to Gerard ter Borch and his legions of followers.

The three-quarter-length composition with the elegant woman in a fur-trimmed jacket pausing in her writing to look at the viewer with the hint of a smile is probably inspired by Johannes Vermeer's *Woman Writing a Letter* in the National Gallery of Art, Washington, D.C. (see cat. 38). However, Metsu retains a more detailed touch and contrasted palette that attest to his origins in the Leiden School and early debt to ter Borch (compare cat. 5). Especially effective is the juxtaposition of the cool color harmonies of the lady's white cowl and powdered visage and the intense red, black, and tan of her costume. Robinson correctly compared the painting with two other works by Metsu depicting elegant ladies seated singly in rich domestic settings, *Woman Making Lace* in the Gemäldegalerie, Dresden, and *Young Woman with a Lapdog* formerly in the collection of the Earl of Ellesmere, Bridgewater House (Robinson 1974, figs. 206, 207). Dating Metsu's works is notoriously difficult owing to his ability to work in more than one style at a time and the paucity of dated works. But these three works seem to fall after his very finely finished *Woman with a Viola da Gamba* of 1663 (Fine Arts Museums of San Francisco) and before the last works of 1667. The present painting bears resemblance in technique to the undated *Doctor's Visit* by Metsu in the Hermitage, St. Petersburg.

–PCS

FRANS VAN MIERIS

(Leiden 1635–1681 Leiden)

Frans van Mieris was born on April 16, 1635, the son of Jansz. Batiaensz., a goldsmith, and Christine Willemsdr. van Garbartijn. He initially followed in his father's profession and was apprenticed in 1647 to his cousin, the goldsmith Willem Fransz. But by 1650 he was a pupil of the glass painter and drawing master Abraham van Toorenvliet. Soon after he began an apprenticeship with Gerard Dou, who later referred to him as the "prince of my pupils." Van Mieris also trained for a period with the Leiden history painter and portraitist Abraham van den Tempel, before returning to Dou's studio. In 1657 he married Cunera van der Cock, with whom he had five children. On May 14, 1658, he entered the Leiden St. Luke's Guild and served as its *hoofdman* (headman) in 1663 and 1664 and its *deken* in 1665. Van Mieris seems to have lived his entire life in Leiden, moving frequently within the city's limits. An extremely successful and popular artist, he was patronized by a number of Leiden's wealthiest and most prominent citizens. He also enjoyed the patronage of foreign nobility, working for Grand Duke Cosimo III de' Medici, who visited him personally in Leiden in 1669, and Archduke Leopold Wilhelm, who unsuccessfully offered him a post as court painter in Vienna. Despite his sizable income, notarial and court documents from the 1660s and 1670s indicate that van Mieris was constantly in debt. The records of unpaid bills at taverns and letters complaining of late delivery of paintings also lend some credence to Arnold Houbraken's claim that the artist was a habitual drunkard. However, van Mieris appears to have been well respected; after his death on March 12, 1681, he was buried alongside prominent Leiden citizens in the St. Pieterskerk.

A leading figure in the Leiden School of *fijnschilders*, van Mieris painted small interior genre scenes, portraits and historical subjects in an extremely detailed and highly refined manner. His style and themes were closely related to those of his teacher Gerard Dou. His meticulous manner was perpetuated by his sons Willem (1662–1747) and Jan (1660–1690), and his grandson Frans van Mieris the Younger (1689–1763). Carel de Moor (1656–1738) was also his pupil and follower.

–PCS

Literature: Hofstede de Groot, vol. 10 (1928); Naumann 1981; exh. cat. Leiden 1988; exh. cat. Amsterdam 1989–90.

Cat. 21.
FRANS VAN MIERIS
A Woman Sealing a Letter by Candlelight
Signed and dated lower right: *1667*
Oil on panel, 27 x 20 cm (arched top)
Private Collection, United States

Provenance: Martin Ascher, before 1970; Fr. Jurgens, Bulkeley House, Englefield Green, England.

Literature: Naumann 1981, vol. 2, p. 131, no. B 10, fig. CB 10 (as either the original or a copy after the painting in Copenhagen); Thierry Beherman, *Godfried Schalcken* (Paris, 1988), p. 362, under no. 338 (under Rejected Attributions).

In a nocturnal interior, a woman in a red fur-trimmed jacket and white cloth hood is seated at a table and illuminated by a bright candle. She holds a letter on the table with her left hand while she melts a stick of sealing wax in the open flame. A young boy, no doubt the messenger, waits to the left to deliver the sealed missive. On the table is an oriental carpet and a small writing desk on which are an inkwell, a slim book, and a second opened letter, to which she evidently responds. In the darkness at the back right is a second woman bringing a candle.

This painting only reemerged last year. Although it had been attributed to Frans van Mieris, it was less well known than a painting in the Royal Museum of Fine Arts, Copenhagen (cat. 1951, no. 648, ill.) that was attributed to the Leiden *fijnschilder* Godfried Schalcken and accepted by, among others, Hofstede de Groot (vol. 5 [1913], no. 263 [as Schalcken]; see Naumann 1981, no. B 10a [as possibly a late work by Frans van Mieris]). In his monograph on Godfried Schalken, Thierry Beherman (1988) rejected the attribution of the work to his artist, improbably suggesting Eglon van der Neer or Pieter van Slingelandt as the possible author. It was not until the present picture resurfaced that Otto Naumann was able to confirm his earlier speculation (based on a photograph) that the present work is the original.

The subject of a woman sealing a letter had been taken up earlier by Gerard ter Borch (see cat. 9). The nocturnal setting had also been a popular setting for women with letters since the subject's conception with Dirck Hals (see cat. 1). However, van Mieris's subtle refinement of the night scene tradition and sophisticated handling of the distribution, cast, and transparency of artificial illumination attest to the legacy of his teacher, Gerard Dou, who was renowned for his minutely executed nocturnes.

–PCS

Cat. 22. (Exhibited in Dublin only)
FRANS VAN MIERIS
A Woman Writing a Letter by Candlelight
Signed and dated lower right: *F van Mieris 1670*
Oil on panel, 16 x 12 cm (arched top)
Private Collection

Provenance: Collection G. J. Cholmondeley, Haigh Hall; with dealer and author John Smith, 1831–42; sale, W. Theobald, London, May 10, 1851, no. 57 (£16.16 to Clark); sale, London, 1881; sale, Palais Galliera, Paris, March, 14, 1972, no. 163, ill. (to David Koetser); David Koetser Gallery, Zurich.

Literature: Smith, *Supplement* (1842), no. 17 (as in the author's own collection); Hofstede de Groot, vol. 10 (1928), no. 164 (1c); Naumann 1981, vol. 1, p. 79, cat. 82, vol. 2, pl. 82.

A young woman in a feathered beret and elegant satin jacket and blouse sits with her head in her hand holding a quill pen to paper. She and her writing instruments are illuminated by an oil lamp with an open flame on the right. Before her on the table is a blank sheet of paper on which she places the nib of her quill, while before her in the lower right is a shadowed inkwell serving as a small but effective *repousssoir*. Her expression is slack, possibly glum, but at very least uninspired.

The pictorial inspiration for this image of a woman writing is again the prototype provided by Gerard ter Borch in the Mauritshuis (cat. 5), which influenced so many painters of the letter theme. However, in that conception of a woman writing a letter, the lady author is depicted working in daylight with great concentration, seemingly inspired. Here, by contrast, the elegantly attired woman works into the night and, putting hand to cheek, seems to suffer, in modern parlance, from writer's block. She stares off into the oblique distance but has not yet written a word. In contrast, her smiling counterpart by van Mieris writes assiduously by candlelight (cat. 23), displaying in the foreground the page of what must be a letter that she has received, since it is creased. She seems fully absorbed in the act of composition and quietly pleased with her writing. In the present painting, the female author has no letter to which to respond. She must initiate the communication and apparently finds the task daunting. Her pose, head in hand, is the traditional pose of Melancholia, which is familiar from antiquity but vividly understood in the Northern pictorial tradition since at least the time of Albrecht Dürer's print of the subject personified by a woman with head in hand. Even the mere composition of a letter could send one into the depths of melancholy.

The present painting probably inspired a painting by Frans van Mieris's student, Carel de Moor, who was in his teacher's workshop during the artist's later period, the date of the present painting, 1670. That work (*fig. 1*) has a similar arched top and was illustrated by Otto Naumann in his monograph on van Mieris (1981, fig. 119), although it remains unlocated. It again depicts an elegantly dressed woman seated in profile at a table composing a letter. The painting offers an image in the highly enameled style of van Mieris's late style and that of his sons and pupils. It also features the amply figured female type that the era favored. She wears many of the same details of costume as the woman in the present work, such as the feathered beret, and has obviously been painted to advertise her stylishness. But she works in daylight, to judge from the forefinger placed to her lips, with reflection and apparent facility.

–PCS

Fig. 1. Carel de Moor
Woman Writing a Letter
Oil on copper, 15 x 11 cm
Location unknown

Cat. 23.
Frans van Mieris
A Young Woman Writing a Letter, c. 1670
Signed lower left
Oil on panel, 18.5 x 14.5 cm
Private Collection, France

Provenance: Possibly sale, Bicker van Zwieten, The Hague, April 12, 1741, no. 64; possibly sale, Crozat, Paris; François Tronchin, cat. 1765, no. 79 (the "first" collection of Tronchin sold en bloc to Catherine II in 1770 for the Hermitage); St. Petersburg cat. 1774, no. 720, cats. 1863–1909, no. 920, cat. 1901, p. 234, no. 920; sold by the Hermitage in 1929; with dealer D. Katz, Dieren, 1938; sale, ten Bos et al., P. Brandt, Amsterdam, April 24, 1959, no. 14, pl. VII (to Ortmann); sale, Christie's, Amsterdam, November 13, 1995, no. 148.

Literature: Hofstede de Groot, vol. 10 (1928), no. 159; Naumann 1981, vol. 1, pp. 79, 111, vol. 2, p. 96, no. 83, ill.

A woman is seated at a table with a writing desk composing a letter with a long quill pen by candlelight. She wears a velvet jacket with fur trim and a white linen cap. Before her, on the extension of the table in the immediate foreground, is a long letter with several prominent creases, indicating that it is one that has been received, not a sheet that she has composed herself. Also before her are writing supplies and, beyond the candle in the candlestick on the desk, an inkwell. The background is shrouded in dark shadow. With her hooded lids and the fingers of her left hand pressed against the paper to steady it as she writes, her expression and pose are all concentration. Yet a faint smile crosses her lips, perhaps in the pleasure of having received such a long letter to which to respond.

This is one of four paintings of letter writers by Frans van Mieris in the present exhibition (see cats. 21–24). In treating letter themes, Mieris, like many other artists, followed in the footsteps of Gerard ter Borch (cat. 5) and probably also those of Gabriel Metsu and Johannes Vermeer in depicting women writing letters. However, he introduced several interesting variations on the subject, including the contemplative, vaguely troubled, possibly tongue-tied author depicted in catalogue 22, as well as the fluent, standing-tall, happy letter writer represented here, and her more compact counterpart in the Rijksmuseum's painting (cat. 24). Here the lengthy letter with tiny, illegible script that rests close by the lady's side, as if for reference as she composes, seems to evoke a principle stressed by Jean Puget de la Serre and other early-seventeenth-century authors of letter-writing

manuals, namely that a letter should respond point by point to the letter received, since its essence is a dialogue and the maintenance of a form of polite, written conversation (see Sutton essay).

To judge from the strong, deeply saturated palette, the full proportions of the figure, and the relatively slick finish of this work, which inclines to an enameled effect rather than the drier touch of van Mieris's earlier works, this is a later painting by the artist. Naumann (1981, p. 79, cat. 83) has plausibly dated it to about 1670 and suggests that it predates the related painting in the Rijksmuseum (cat. 24), which is dated ten years later. The latter depicts a similarly conceived lady writing a letter in profile, half-length, but omits the useful letter in the foreground and adds a young messenger, as well as details like a lute and sleeping lapdog. A fine example of van Mieris's mature art, this work was appreciated by a remarkably august group of collectors, including François Tronchin and Catherine the Great of Russia, for whom it was acquired for the Hermitage (sold 1929). It also may have been owned by the distinguished eighteenth century Hague collector Bicker van Zwieten and the famous Parisian connoisseur Pierre Crozat. An earlier provenance (assumed by Hofstede de Groot, no. 159, to refer to the present work) in the J. van der Marck collection, sold in Amsterdam in 1773, seems, despite correspondence in dimensions and description, to refer to another painting, since it postdates Catherine's acquisition of the present work in 1770.

–PCS

Cat. 24.
FRANS VAN MIERIS
A Woman Writing a Letter
Signed and dated upper left: *F van Mieris fecit Anno 1680*
Oil on panel, 25 x 19.5 cm
Rijksmuseum, Amsterdam, inv. no. SK-A-261

Provenance: Sale, D. Grenier, Middelburg, August 18, 1712, no. 122 (for 151 fl.); C. Reygersbergen van Cauwerven Collection, Middelburg, 1760; his sale, Leiden, July 31, 1765, no. 30 (for 2,100 fl. to Yver for Braamcamp); sale, G. Bramcamp, Amsterdam, July 31, 1771, no. 135 (3,610 fl. to Fouquet); sale, Randon de Boisset, Paris, February 3, 1777, no. 125; sale, Beaujon, Paris (Remy, Julliot; Boileau; Girardin), April 25, 1787, no. 65 (7,002 francs to Lebrun); Destouches, 1792; his sale, Paris, May 24, 1794, no. 46 (1,000 francs); Notary H. van Wel Collection, Brussels; bought with a painting by van der Werff from Wel by van der Pot (for 1926.4 fl.) 1795; sale, van der Pot van Groeneveld, Rotterdam, June 6, 1808, no. 76 (2025 fl. to Jorissen for the Rijksmuseum).

Exhibitions: Leiden, Stedelijk Museum De Lakenhal, *Leidse Fijnschilders: Van Gerrit Dou tot Frans van Mieris de Jonge 1630–1760*, 1988, no. 27, ill.; Amsterdam/Tokyo 1991–92, Amsterdam, Rijksmuseum, Tokyo, Suntory Museum of Art, *Japanese Influence on Dutch Art: Imitation and Inspiration from 1650 to the Present*, 1991–92, no. 57, ill. in color.

Literature: J. B. Descamps, *La vie des peintres flamands, allemands et hollandais*, 4 vols. (Paris, 1753–63), vol. 3, p. 22; J. P. B. Lebrun, *Galerie des peintres flamands, hollandais et allemands*, 3 vols. (Paris, 1792–96), vol. 2, p. 22; Smith, vol. 1 (1829), no. 31; W. Bürger [T. Thoré], *Musées de la Hollande*, vol. 1, *Amsterdam et La Haye* (Paris, 1858), p. 89; C. Blanc, *Histoire des peintres de toutes les écoles*, vol. 10, *Ecole hollandaise* (Paris, 1863), vol. 2, p. 23; "Frans van Mieries, de oude 1635–1681," *De Vlaamsche School* 26 (1880), p. 140; Hofstede de Groot, vol. 10 (1928), no. 157; E. W. Moes and E. van Biema, *De nationale Konstgallerij en het Koninklijk Museum: bijdrage tot de geschiedenis van het Rijksmuseum* (Amsterdam, 1909), pp. 11, 183; A. Brunt, "F. van Mieries en zijn werken in onze Hollandsche verzamelingen," *Morks Magazijn* 13 (1911), p. 37, ill. p. 39; A. Masson, "La galerie Beaujon," *Gazette des Beaux-Arts*, ser. 6, 18 (1937), p. 53; W. Martin, *Dutch Painting of the Great Period, 1650–1697*, trans. P. Horning (London, 1950), p. 87, no. 192, ill.; Bénézit, vol. 6, p. 117; Gudlaugsson 1959–60, vol. 2, p. 121, pl. VIII, fig. 2; Bille 1961, vol. 1, p. 74, ill., vol. 2, p. 106, no. 135; S. J. Gudlaugsson, "Frans van Mieris d.A.," *Kindlers Lexikon*

(Zurich, 1967), p. 422; exh. cat. Amsterdam 1976, p. 387; Otto Naumann, "Frans van Mieris as a Draughtsman," *Master Drawings* 16, no. 1 (1978), p. 22 n. 36; Naumann 1981, vol. 1, p. 111, vol. 2, p. 123, no. 118, ill.; S. van Raay, *Imitation and Inspiration: Japanese Influence on Dutch Art* (Amsterdam, 1989), fig. 5, in color.

Seated at a table in a dark domestic interior, a serene, richly attired lady facing left and shown half-length pens a letter on an unfolded sheet of paper. Dominating the center of the composition, she is the most brightly lit element, her plain white inner cap with an openwork border, gleaming golden brown wadded *Japonsche rok* (dressing gown) over a white undergown, and white quill commanding the beholder's attention. To her left a less finely rendered brown-haired male page, wearing a white cravat and with purple ribbons at his shoulder, patiently and respectfully awaits the missive, without intruding on the writer's privacy. An overturned lute occupies a third of the table—covered with a sumptuous purplish velvet tablecloth—at the left, while the letter writer and her instruments (quill, inkstand, and paper) take up the right. The act of letter writing is the compositional focus, framed by the woman's hand, that of the page, the lute's pegbox, and the inkstand. Before the table on an olive-green velvet stool is a sleeping miniature spaniel. A view into another, brighter room in a classicizing style opens up at the right.

Painted in 1680, this is one of van Mieris's last works and typifies his late style in its marked interest in reflections on shimmering fabric and hard surfaces, a smooth, porcelain-like finish, and a disregard for the anatomy of his figures. While creating new compositions, he nevertheless repeated certain details. For instance, a similar dressing gown is found in the 1679 *Death of Lucretia* (Private Collection, Sweden; Naumann 1981, no. 116). Moreover, the curled-up spaniel is a direct quotation of the dog in the 1671 *Song Interrupted* (Petit Palais, Paris; Naumann 1981, no. 88) and is found in reverse in *Concert of Six Figures* (present location unknown; Naumann 1981, no. 103) and *The Holy Family* of 1681 (present location unknown; Naumann 1981, no. 121). Spaniels in such a position relate to two lost animal studies by van Mieris that were recorded in a print by Ploos van Amstel (see Naumann 1978 , p. 31, nos. 26, 27, pls. 21a, 21b, especially no. 26 of a dog sleeping on a chair).

Van Mieris had addressed the theme of a woman writing a letter on two other occasions approximately a decade earlier: *A Lady Writing a Letter by Candlelight*, 1670 (cat. 22) and *A Young Woman Writing a Letter*, about 1670 (cat. 23). The former painting portrays a woman lost in contemplation, deliberating over her writing, alone, and

144   *Cat. 24, detail*

with few accessories. The second work presents a young woman replying to a letter she has received in a somewhat more detailed setting. Both are also nocturnal scenes. The Rijksmuseum painting is an expanded narrative of the first two, and the most compositionally complex.

Van Mieris was relying on several traditions. For nocturnal scenes, he had the example of another *fijnschilder*, Gerard Dou, who popularized such paintings earlier in the seventeenth century (informed in turn by artists such as Rembrandt and the Dutch Caravaggisti). For women writing letters, van Mieris turned to Gerard ter Borch, arguably the theme's greatest proponent by midcentury, whose *Woman Writing a Letter* of about 1655 (cat. 5) may have been van Mieris's immediate source of inspiration in terms of composition. Van Mieris's highly polished technique and contrasts of light, naturally, differ.

The contemporary viewer may well have understood the lady in the Rijksmuseum as writing a love letter. As Naumann and others have pointed out, these compositions highlighted the moral dilemma faced by women writing such billets-doux, which could have dire legal and social consequences. While we do not know to whom the letter is addressed, the presence of its recipient is suggested by the upside-down lute. Van Mieris used this same device in his *Woman Singing* of about 1679 (present location unknown; Naumann 1981, no. 86), whose compositional structure, table, figures shown *en trois-quart*, and classicizing setting are not far removed from those in the painting under discussion. The lute, moreover, could evoke any number of associations, from harmony in marriage to a lack of chastity or female genitalia, or serve as an attribute of prostitutes (Amsterdam 1976, no. 21), and love. Here it probably stands more generally for the one with whom the woman hopes to "make music." The sensuality of the subject matter would seem to be underscored by van Mieris's delight in rendering the gleaming stuffs, the silken texture of the lute and the dog's coat, and the soft, smooth skin of the lady's décolleté.

Her casual yet sumptuous attire merits a note. The silk wadded gown was an unusual item of clothing. Its origins lie in the gifts of padded silk kimonos made by the Japanese shogun to officials of the Dutch East India Company. In turn, the *Japonsche rokken* were increasingly used as gifts by the Heeren XVII, representatives of the Dutch East India Company. However, the supply of *schenkagierocken* (gift gowns) soon fell short of demand, and the company was eventually granted permission to order them from the Japanese tailors' guild. Highly prized in the Netherlands and specially traded by the Dutch East India Company, these *robes de chambre* were usually worn by men, though women sometimes donned them,

as documented in inventories and depicted in paintings (van Raay 1989, pp. 53–59). Constantijn Huygens even wrote about this upper-class finery in his *Korenbloemen (Cornflowers)* (1658):

> I liken Kitty to Japanese wadding,
> Either in virtue or in weight,
> For both Kitty and wadding are very warm and
> very light.

> —JK

Cat. 25.
FRANS VAN MIERIS
The Matchmaker (Bathsheba)
Signed and dated lower left: *F. van Mieris fect/Anno 1671*
Oil on panel, 29.5 x 24 cm
Gemäldegalerie Alte Meister, Staatliche
Kunstsammlungen Dresden, inv. no. 1742

Provenance: Acquired from de Wit, a dealer in Antwerp,
1710; first recorded in the Dresden inventory of 1722.

Exhibition: East Berlin, Bode Museum (an exhibition of
paintings from Dresden), 1955–56, p. 114.

Literature: Charles Blanc, *Histoire des peintres de toutes les
écoles. École Hollandaise* (Paris, 1863), vol. 2, pp. 2, 23, with
an engraved illustration; Plietzsch 1960, p. 54; Naumann
1981, vol. 1, pp. 82–83, 116, vol. 2, pp. 99–100, pl. 87.

An elegantly attired young woman sits in profile at
a table with her right arm draped over the chair back
holding a letter, her left arm resting on the table and
cupping her chin. Her graceful form is relaxed; the
action of her crossed legs reveals a slipper that emerges
from her ample slate blue silk skirt. Her jacket is a
rich orange-yellow, and her hair is braided and coiled
neatly at the back of her head. She seems to listen in a
desultory fashion to an old woman sitting on the far side
of the table who smiles toothlessly and gestures with her
figures, as if enumerating points. The table is covered in
green velvet, on which rests a lute. In the right distance
the scene opens onto a balustrade and tall, open arches
with trees beyond, suggesting a palatial setting. In the
shadows at the back left is a large altarlike piece of
furniture. In the lower left foreground sits a small
spaniel dog.

The painting is a mature work by Frans van Mieris
painted one year after his *Letter Writer* of 1670 (cat. 22),
which also depicts a woman with head in hand but in
a very different emotional state. While the latter seems
troubled by her writing task, here the recipient of the
letter is at her ease, casually comfortable. Although
typically composed on a small scale and employing a
highly refined, detailed execution, van Mieris's painting
adopts a full-length, profile composition that enables him
to maximize the effect of sensual languor in the woman's
enervated body language. When the painting was first
catalogued in the Dresden inventories in 1722 it was
described in neutrally descriptive terms as a "Lady
Conversing with an Old Woman" (*eine Dame redet mit
einer alten Frau*). Although no inscription is now visible
in the picture, Naumann noted (1981, vol. 2, p. 99) that
Charles Blanc in 1863 recorded the appearance of the

word AMOR on the piece of furniture at the back left,
which suggests that the letter the lady holds could well
be a love letter. Blanc further identified the young lady
as a courtesan. As Naumann observed (vol. 1, p. 116), the
presence of the old woman conforming to a procuress
type (see Sutton essay) suggests that the subject is the
Old Testament theme of Bathsheba's receipt of King
David's letter. In his conception of the comfortable and
malleable Bathsheba, van Mieris implies that she will
succumb to the letter's temptation and the procuress's
blandishments. Thus his treatment of the theme is
conceptually allied in its iconography with that of his old
friend, Jan Steen (cat. 31), who also depicted Bathsheba
in contemporary costume and as a receptive partner in
the seduction. Plietzsch (1960) and Naumann even
observed that the execution of the present work, with
its spirited treatment of the lady's elegant attire, resembles
Steen's style and brushwork. Since Steen's *Bathsheba* is
usually dated about 1659–61, when the impact of ter
Borch's art was most apparent in his work, it is likely
that he preceded and inspired van Mieris in this case,
but the dialogue between the two masters was lasting
and mutually beneficial.

–PCS

Cat. 26.
FRANS VAN MIERIS
Woman with a Lapdog and an Old Woman
Signed and dated: *1680*
Oil on panel, 19.1 x 15.1 cm
Private Collection, The Netherlands

Provenance: Sale, G. Bicker van Zwieten, The Hague, April 12, 1731, no. 57; sale, A. Bout, The Hague, August 11, 1733, no. 54; sale, G. Bicker van Zwieten, The Hague, April 4, 1755, no. 24; sale, Van Campen, Amsterdam, August 2, 1830, no. 52; sale, Alexander Boyle, London, June 25, 1898, no. 68; sale, Hôtel Drouot, Paris, June 13, 1997, no. 48; purchased from Salomon Lilian, 2003.

Literature: Hofstede de Groot, vol. 10 (1928), p. 59, no. 227; *Salomon Lilian. Old Masters 2003* (Amsterdam, 2003), pp. 48–49, cat. 16, ill.

A young woman in a green velvet jacket, plunging décolleté, and gold skirt is seated next to a table with a red cover and a still life composed of an opened letter with a red seal, an orange, and a glass vase or carafe, possibly of wine, closed with a paper stopper. She has a small papillon spaniel in her lap and combs her long brunette hair. A smiling old crone dressed in black behind her chatters in her ear. At the back right is a sculpture of a putto on a dolphin.

This only recently rediscovered work is dated 1680, like the *Letter Writer* from the Rijksmuseum (cat. 24), and employs the figure types, strong palette, and enameled technique of van Mieris's late works. The lady is engaged in her toilette, combing her long hair, like the woman in van Mieris's painting of just two years earlier in the Louvre (Naumann 1981, cat. 114). However, in this instance she also has an opened letter on her dressing table, like the young woman in the painting of 1667 in the museum in Dresden (Naumann 1981, vol. 2, pl. 69). As Naumann has pointed out (1981, p. 113), open letters also appear inconspicuously on the dressing tables in *Woman with a Dancing Dog* in the Hermitage (Naumann 1981, cat. 32) and *Woman Admiring Herself in a Mirror* in Berlin (Sutton essay, *fig. 42*; Naumann 1981, cat. 46), both from the early 1660s, and seem to be associated in van Mieris's mind with the rarefied, self-absorbed lives and vanity of privileged women. In the present case, the young woman is accompanied by a wizened old woman, with sunken and projecting features and grayish green complexion, who resembles the procuress types whom van Mieris (see cat. 25) and other Dutch artists, such as Jan Steen (cat. 31), depict in their "modern" history paintings on the subject of Bathsheba. Frans van Mieris was closely allied with Jan Steen during their years

together in Leiden and perhaps shared the latter's view of Bathsheba as a willing recipient of King David's letter (see Sutton essay). Given the presence of the letter and the statue of the frolicking putto at the back, love is surely in the air, and the old woman's blandishments, considered within the pictorial tradition, suggest that the letter brings not only love but illicit temptation.

–PCS

NICOLAS KNÜPFER

(Leipzig c. 1609–1655 Utrecht)

Nicolas Knüpfer was born in Leipzig, Germany, where he was apprenticed to the local artist, Emanuel Nysse. The artist's date of birth has not been pinpointed, but a recently published document gave his age as "about 30" in 1639. As a youth, he moved to Magdeburg, where he was active as both a brush maker and painter before traveling to Utrecht at the age of twenty-six. The inscription on Pieter de Jode's engraving of Knüpfer's portrait published by Johannes Meijssens in 1649 states that he went to Utrecht to work with Abraham Bloemaert. Cornelis de Bie (1661) also describes him as an assistant in Bloemaert's studio. When he registered in the Utrecht St. Luke's Guild in 1637, he was a "visiting" painter, suggesting he was only planning a temporary stay; however, he remained there until his death. In November 1640 he married Cornelia Beck in a civil ceremony. Although their marriage survived fewer than three years before Cornelia died, they had two children. Knüpfer took part in the Utrecht School's contributions to the illustrated history of Denmark for the decorations of Kronberg Castle. Knüpfer also sold works to King Charles I of England in 1650. He also painted *The Pursuit of Pleasure (Il Contento)* in 1651 for the collector Willem Vincent, baron van Wyttenhorst. Despite his successes, Knüpfer died penniless in 1655 in his parents' house on the Neude before October 15, 1655. His son, who was apprenticed as a goldsmith, survived him by only five years. Knüpfer had students, including the little-known Pieter Crijnsen Volmarijn as well as the famous comedic artist, Jan Steen. Notwithstanding his minimal estate, he was purported to be able to charge his students seventy-two guilders per year.

Nicolaus Knüpfer was active as a history and genre painter. His genre scenes are far less numerous than his history paintings, which are stylistically and thematically original and highly animated.

–PCS

Literature: Juri Kuznetsov, "Nikolaus Knüpfer (1603?–1655)," *Oud Holland* 88 (1974), pp. 168–219; exh. cat. The Walters Art Gallery, Baltimore, and the Fine Arts Museums of San Francisco, *Masters of Light: Dutch Painters in Utrecht during the Golden Age*, 1997–98; Jo Saxton (dissertation).

Cat. 27.
NICOLAS KNÜPFER
Sophonisba Holding a Letter
Signed lower right: *Nknupfer*
Oil on panel, 24.2 x 21.3 cm
Private Collection, UK

Provenance: Sale Jan de Bondt, Wijk bij Duurstede, 1649, no. 20; Ferdinand Graf von Plettenberg (1690 – 1737); Schloss Nordkirchen; Maria Anna von Galen, 1737 – 1771; Freiherren von Ketteler, Schlösser Schwarzenraben und Harkotten, 1771 – 1999

Literature: Juri I. Kuznetsov, Nicolaus Knüpfer (1603? – 1655)," in *Oud Holland*, vol. 88 (1974), pp. 168 – 219, no. 123a; Markus Kamps, "Sammlung Plettenberg, Glanz und Niedergang im 18. Jahrhundert in Westfalen," *Weltkunst*, April 4, 1999, pp. 684 – 96; Jo Saxton, "An Original Artist; Nicolaus Knupfer (Leipzig ca.1605 – Utrecht 1655)," Ph.D. dissertation, Institute of Fine Arts, New York, 2003, cat. A66.

A woman in a gold dress with décolleté, knotted sash and blue mantle swoons, her eyes rolling heavenward, as she sits in a throne-like chair. She has tight curls, large pearl earrings and holds a letter in her right hand. Her right foot still rests on a foot warmer. Behind her on a table is a covered cup, a crown and a gold chain. An old woman looks in at the door at the back left and raises her hand in alarm.

This painting appears outwardly to be little more than another secular letter subject depicting a woman expressing anxiety or grief over the receipt of a letter with unwelcome news (compare Sutton essay, *fig. 2*, and cat. 12), but in this case the subject is taken from Roman history. The scene depicts the demise of Sophonisba, recounted by Livy (XXX:15), who was the beautiful and fatefully seductive daughter of the Carthaginian general, Hasdrubal, during the second Punic war. She married a Numidian prince and turned him against his Roman masters. He was captured by another Numidian leader loyal to the Romans, Masinissa. The Roman general, Scipio, demanded that Sophonisba be turned over and delivered to Rome with her captured husband. However before she could be arrested she threw herself at Masinissa, who succumbed immediately to Sophonisba's charms and granted her entreaty that he would not send her to Rome. Smitten, he impetuously married her the same day. For defying the general, Massinissa was summoned by Scipio, who was renowned for his own personal continence, having declined a woman as human plunder on his own Carthaginian campaign in Spain. Scipio observed to Masinissa, "There is no danger so

the same year, 1671, formerly in Bridgewater House (see cat. 30, *fig. 1*), in the later painting of 168[0?] in Rotterdam (cat. 30), and in several other paintings, including a *Lawyer Sharpening a Quill Pen* in the Nationalmuseum, Stockholm, no. 551 (Hofstede de Groot, vol. 3 [1910], no. 73). The theme and composition, with the seated lawyer in a cap turning away from a cluttered desk as he reads, was treated three years earlier by Ostade in a painting signed and dated 1668 that was with Brod Gallery in London in 1957.

On the history of depicting lawyers in Northern genre scenes and Ostade's particular interpretation of that tradition, see catalogue 30.

—PCS

Cat. 29. (Exhibited in Dublin only)
ADRIAEN VAN OSTADE
A Lawyer Reading a Letter or Document in his Office
Signed and dated: *167[7 or 1]*
Oil on panel, 36.7 x 30.4 cm
Collection Marquis of Bute

Provenance: Sale, F. W. Baron von Borck, Amsterdam, May 1, 1771, no. 7, to C. Fouquet; marquis of Bute, by 1829 (see Smith).

Exhibition: Edinburgh, National Gallery of Scotland, *Dutch and Flemish Paintings from the Collection of the Marquis of Bute*, 1949, no. 35.

Literature: Smith, vol. 1 (1829), no. 48; Waagen, vol. 3 (1854), p. 478; P. Richter, *Catalogue of the Collection . . . of the Marquis of Bute*, (London, 1884), no. 125; Hofstede de Groot, vol. 3 (1910), no. 68.

Engraved: By Beauvarlet as *Le Bourgmestre.*

A man is seated in a cluttered office with his head in hand reading a letter or document. His narrow-brimmed hat is cocked to one side as he puts fist to cheek in a casual, self-forgetful attitude of concentration. He wears spectacles, a goatee, a short ruffled collar, and the tabard often worn by lawyers and other professionals (see cat. 30). While the subject was assumed to be a burgomaster when engraved by Beauvarlet, his costume and accessories verify that he is a lawyer. On the carpet-covered desk before him are books and papers, some with official seals, as well as an inkwell with a quill. Deeds and other papers are pinned together and gathered in pouches hanging from the wall. There are rows of books in shelves as well as a reading stand with books behind him on the right.

Lawyers were one of Adriaen van Ostade's favorite subjects for his paintings of professionals, especially in his later career. Like notaries and professional secretaries, lawyers were often employed to read or write official letters for private individuals, usually on a legal, business, or professional matter. They also were men of considerable social standing in Dutch society (see G. D. J. Schotel 1905, *Het maatschappelijk leven onzer vaderen in de zeventiende eeuw* [Arnhem, 1905], pp. 380–82) but often were depicted in the pictorial tradition of genre painting as comically abusive figures (see Sutton essay, *figs. 17 & 18*). In Ostade's paintings, lawyers usually are depicted as men reading documents or letters and surrounded by books and papers in a cluttered office. Ostade had earlier painted seated lawyers singly, half- to three-quarter-length, in similar costumes reading; see, for example, the

painting dated 1665, which may depict the same model, in the Louvre (*fig. 1*; Hofstede de Groot, vol. 3, no. 85), and the undated painting formerly in Fonthill Abbey (Hofstede de Groot, vol. 3, no. 75). Although the date on the present work has been read as 1677, it may be 1671, which is the same as on the paintings of lawyers in Sudeley Castle and formerly in Bridgewater House (see cat. 28 and cat 30, *fig. 1*). The painting exhibited here from Rotterdam is a later work, dating from the last five years of Ostade's career, and depicts an older, heavier-set gentleman. However, as in that work, Ostade here presents the lawyer as respectable and hardworking, if a bit disorderly in his filing habits, as was the custom in depicting the profession. The attention in the present work to the details of the still-life accessories, the textures of different fabrics, parchment and paper, indeed even of the rather rumpled-looking lawyer himself, lends the work a compelling naturalism that is consummately Dutch in its dedication to a minute record of a commonplace, undramatic subject.

–PCS

Fig. 1. Adriaen van Ostade
Lawyer Reading
Signed and dated: *1665*
Oil on panel, 10 x 16 cm
Musée du Louvre, Paris, no. MI 945

Cat. 30
ADRIAEN VAN OSTADE
A Lawyer with a Letter or Document in his Study
Signed and dated on the letter: *AvOstade 168(?)*
Oil on panel, 34.5 x 28 cm
Museum Boijmans Van Beuningen, Rotterdam, no. 1637

Provenance: Possibly in the collection of Paslin or
Choiseul, Paris; sale, Paillet and Delaroche, Paris, May 30,
1799, no. 72, sold to Perrier for 307 livres; F. J. O.
Boymans Collection, Utrecht, 1811; bequeathed by F. J.
O. Boymans to the museum in 1847.

Literature: *Catalogue d'un magifique cabinet de tableaux, de
plus célèbres maîtres des trios écoles . . . Le tout depuis nombre
d'années rassemblé[s] par Monsieur F. J. O. Boymans*
(Amsterdam, August 1811), p. 44, no. B 72; *Catalogus van
schilderijen enz. In het Museum te Rotterdam gesticht door Mr.
F. J. O. Boymans*, 1849, no. 211; Hofstede de Groot, vol. 3
(1910), no. 74; W. Martin, *De schilderkunst in de tweede helft
van de zeventiende eeuw* (Amsterdam, 1950), p. 83, no. 169;
Friso Lammertse, *Dutch Genre Paintings of the 17th
Century. Collection of the Museum Boijmans van Beuningen*
(Rotterdam, 1998), pp. 134–35, no. 45, ill.

Seated at a desk, a lawyer holds a handwritten
letter or document in his left hand and his spectacles in
his right. He is an elderly, stout gentleman with white
hair and mustache and the earnest expression of
concentration. Viewed at three-quarter-length, the lawyer
wears a violet tabard over black clothes and has a black
cap. The table is covered with an oriental carpet and
piled high with books, writing supplies, and other sealed
documents and papers. Papers, books, and ledgers also
appear on the floor, on a shelf at the back, and hang from
pegs in the wall beyond a blue screen. At the back left is
an open door leading to a hallway with a window.

Although sometimes identified simply as an old man
or even a philosopher, the subject has been correctly
identified by Friso Lammertse (1998, p. 135) as a lawyer,
based on the violet tabard that he wears. While tabards
had gone out of fashion among the general public by the
time this picture was painted, they were still associated
with some occupations, notably church ministers,
scientists, and members of the legal profession (see M. de
Winkel, "'Eene der deftigsten dragten': The Iconography
of the Tabbaard and the Sense of Tradition in Dutch
Seventeenth-Dentury Portraiture," in *Beeld en zelfbeeld
in de Nederlandse kunst 1550–1750, Nederlandse
Kunsthistorisch Jaarboek* 46 [1995], pp. 145–67). Lawyers
were often depicted surrounded with sheaves of papers
and filing pouches. Ostade painted many images of
lawyers, especially in his later career; Hofstede de Groot

Fig. 1. Adriaen van Ostade
Lawyer with a Letter and a Client
Signed and dated lower left: *A. Ostade 1671*
Oil on panel, 31 x 26.2 cm
Formerly Earl of Ellesmere, Bridgewater House, London

(vol. 3, nos. 67–77c), listed no fewer than nineteen pictures of this subject (see also cats. 28 & 29). The painting is closest in conception to two other three-quarter-length paintings of lawyers at their desks, also holding a letter or document and surrounded with books and papers, both dated 1671, one in the Morrison collection, Sudeley Castle, Gloucestershire (cat. 28), and the other formerly in the earl of Ellesmere's collection in Bridgewater House, London (*fig. 1*; respectively Hofstede de Groot, vol. 3, nos. 69 and 67). Indeed, all three paintings seem to have employed the same model. In the Bridgewater House painting, the lawyer has a client who, true to the pictorial tradition, is an anxious-looking peasant who respectfully doffs his cap and holds a dead woodcock, no doubt to barter for the legal advice. As noted in the Introduction, the tradition of depicting lawyers descends from sixteenth century peasant painting traditions (see Georges Marlier, *Pierre Brueghel le Jeune* [Brussels, 1969], pp. 435–40, in which he lists no fewer than 39 versions of a composition, possible first conceived by Pieter Bruegel the Elder, depicting peasants lining up in a lawyer's paper-strewn office with their barter items). However, even in the Ellesmere painting, Ostade departs from the satirical tradition of representing the subject, treating both the lawyer and his client with respect and dignity.

Lammertse (1998) has also pointed out the present picture's close resemblance to a painting dated 1681 by Ostade in the Hermitage, St. Petersburg, of a lawyer reading a letter that is the personification of Sight in series of the Five Senses (three of the original five panels survive, Hermitage, nos. 956–58). Ostade seems to have been the first artist to depict Sight as a lawyer scrutinizing a paper. Thus the present work may also have once been part of a Five Senses series, but the other works in the hypothetical series have not been identified. Although the final digit of the date is no longer legible, this painting must have been executed in the last five years of the artist's life when he was already seventy years old, though clearly still in command of his artistic skills.

–PCS

JAN STEEN
(Leiden 1626–1679 Leiden)

Jan Steen was born in Leiden, the son of a brewer. His date of birth has not been pinpointed, but in 1646, when he matriculated at Leiden University, he was recorded as being twenty years old. Arnold Houbraken claimed that he was a pupil of the landscapist Jan van Goyen, whose daughter he married. J. D. Weyerman further claimed that Steen studied successively with Nicholas Knüpfer (q.v.) at Utrecht, Adriaen van Ostade (q.v.) at Haarlem, and finally with van Goyen in The Hague. Steen is recorded in Leiden between 1644 and 1646. In March 1648 he became a member of the newly founded St. Luke's Guild in Leiden, proving that by this date he had become an independent master. By September 1649 he was living in The Hague and was married there to Margarethe van Goyen. Although he was still living in The Hague in July 1654, in April 1653 he paid dues to the Leiden guild. His father leased a brewery for him in Delft from 1654 to 1657, and he painted a Delft scene in 1655, but there is no proof that he ever resided or remained long in that city. From 1656 to 1660 he was living in a small house in Warmond, near Leiden. By 1661 he had settled in Haarlem, where he entered the guild and eventually remained until 1670, when he inherited a house in Leiden. He then remained in his native city until the end of his life. Steen applied for permission to open an inn in 1672. He served as *hoofdman*, or leader of the guild, in 1671, 1672, and 1673, and as *deken* in 1674. He was buried in Leiden on 3 February 1679.

Although known chiefly for his humorous genre scenes, Steen also painted religious, mythological and historical subjects. His art reveals knowledge of contemporary literature and theater. Although recent studies have reduced the size of his large oeuvre, he was an exceptionally prolific artist.

–PCS

Literature: Tobias van Westreheene, *Jan Steen: Etude sur l'art en Hollande* (The Hague, 1856); Hofstede de Groot, vol. 1 (1907), pp. 1–252; A. Bredius, *Jan Steen* (Amsterdam, 1927); F. Schmidt-Degener, *Jan Steen* (London, 1927); Kirschenbaum 1977; Braun 1980; exh. cat. Washington/Amsterdam 1996–97; Westermann 1997.

Cat. 31. (Exhibited in Greenwich only)
JAN STEEN
Bathsheba with King David's Letter, 1659-60
Signed above the door
Oil on panel, 41.5 x 33 cm
Private Collection

Provenance: Sale, J. Enschede, Haarlem, May 30, 1786, no. 16; sale, P. Lyonet, Amsterdam, April 11, 1791, no. 232; probably sale, Henry et al., Paris, April 9, 1822, no. 67 (described as a genre scene); sale, Susanna de Bosch, née de Vries, Amsterdam, November 3, 1840, no. 102 (as on canvas and "by or after" Jan Steen; 50 fl. to de Lelie); possibly sale, van Saceghem of Ghent, Brussels, June 2, 1851, no. 60 (but as 18 x 15 in.; 2600 francs to de Roy); sale, Théodore Patureau, Paris, April 20, 1857, no. 34; Lord Powerscourt, at Powerscourt; Prince Liechtenstein, Vienna, 1907; Princess Murat, Paris, 1911; with dealer Knoedler, New York, 1926; with Colnaghi's, London, 1935; E. Nicholas, Paris, sold to Edward Speelman, London, by 1977; private collection, Great Britain; acquired by the present owner about 1980.

Exhibitions: London, Royal Academy of Arts, Winter Exhibition, 1878, no. 123 (as *Le Billet Doux*); New York, National Academy of Design, *Dutch and Flemish Paintings from New York Private Collections*, cat. by Ann Jensen Adams, 1988, no. 47, ill.; Washington/Amsterdam 1996–97, no. 11, ill.

Literature: Hofstede de Groot, vol. 1 (1907), no. 15; Bredius 1927; C. W. de Groot, 1952, p. 123; de Vries 1977, pp. 49, 54, 161, no. 88; Kirschenbaum 1977, pp. 40, 116–17; Braun 1980, p. 100, no. 110, ill.; Naumann 1981, vol. 1 pp. 115–16; Westermann 1997, pp. 216, 289, fig. 124.

In an elegant interior, a young and an old woman face each other. Wearing a yellow bodice and red skirt, the young woman stands in profile but turns her head to look directly at the viewer. She holds up a letter to display it. Dressed in black with a black headdress, the old woman is bent over and walks with a cane. She evidently has just delivered the letter and gestures to the young woman. At the back left there is a chair with a candle and a chamber pot, and against the wall a covered bed. The walls are decorated with gilt leather. Through an open door at the back right is a view of a palace with gardens, through which walks a gentleman dressed in a red cloak.

Although the figures both wear seventeenth-century costume and the furnishings are of the period, the letter identifies the subject as the Old Testament theme of

Cat. 33.
JAN STEEN
Bordello Scene (Bathsheba?), c. 1665–68
Signed above the door: *Ian Steen*
Oil on panel, 61.6 x 46 cm
Szépmüvészeti Múzeum, Budapest (Museum of Fine
Arts, Budapest), inv. no. 4300

Provenance: Sale, Amsterdam August 10, 1785, to
Wubbels; sold by Nestcher to Klerk de Reus, The
Hague; de Reus collection acquired by M. von
Rothschild, Frankfurt; sold by G. Plach, Vienna, to Graf
Johann Pálffy, Bratislava, 1869; bequeathed to the
museum, 1912.

Exhibitions: Cologne, Wallraf-Richartz Museum, and
Utrecht Centraal Museum, *Niederländische Malerei des 17.
Jahrhunderts aus Budapest,* 1987, no. 37, ill.; Frankfurt
1993, no. 77, ill.

Literature: Smith, *Supplement* (1844), no. 105; Hofstede
de Groot, vol. 1 (1907), no. 826; Braun 1980, no. 336;
Westermann 1997, p. 291 n. 41, fig. 170.

In a shadowed interior a young woman in a gold silk
skirt and bodice with lavender jacket reclines tipsily in a
chair holding up a glass of wine in one hand and a letter
in the other. She rests her elbow on a crimson pillow on
top of a chair in which a small lapdog sleeps. Her right
foot is perched on a foot warmer, and a wine cooler
with vessels appears on the floor at the lower right.
Behind her is a table covered with an oriental carpet, a
pewter pitcher, and tall flute glass. A glass sphere hangs
from the ceiling by a ribbon, while on the back wall is a
painting in a gold frame of the Prodigal Son Driven from
the Whorehouse, which features, as often was depicted in
illustrations of this biblical parable, the madame wielding

a broom. At the back right an old woman, undoubtedly
the procuress, in black with a cane, admits a young man
in a cape and beribboned hat who places coins in her
hand. The arched doorway above is decorated with a
putto and gilt grapevines, while a lute and wall clock
hang farther back. In the shadows at the back left is
a canopied bed.

As if the young lady's feather headdress, abundant
décolleté, drunken demeanor, and lascivious smile were
not explicit enough, the transaction in the doorway at
the back certifies that the painting depicts a prostitute
in a brothel. The moral message of the parable of the
Prodigal Son is made universal by the reflecting globe
overhead, which in emblems of the period is a symbol
of God's omniscience. The clock also can be seen as an
admonition to heed the transience of life. Thus, the
painting's message seems to be, reject the wasteful life
of sensual pleasure personified by the Prodigal Son
and make a timely start on your salvation.

There is writing on the letter the woman holds that
has been the subject of considerable discussion. Most
recently Mariët Westermann, like others before her, saw
in the only partially legible letters the beginning of the
name ("Berse . . .") Bath[sheba]; thus, the painting would
be another example of Steen's treating this popular
history painting subject in the guise of genre (compare
cat. 31). She felt that catalogue 31 was Steen's "most
explicit and modern comment on Bathsheba's status as
a willing accomplice [with King David in their affair]"
(1997) But Karel Braun (1980) and E. Mai (in
Cologne/Utrecht 1987) have questioned whether the
letters spell "Bathsheba" and not "*Berke* [or] *Birke van. . .
.*" The authors of the catalogue accompanying the
exhibition *Leselust,* held in Frankfurt in 1993, argued
instead that the prostitute with the letter alluded to the
fact that letters were often used by courtesans in their
venal transactions with clients. A print from Crispijn de
Passe's multilingual and highly popular *Miroir des plus
belles Courtisanes de ce Temps; Spiegel der aderschoonste
Coutesanen deser tyts* (The looking-glass of the fairest
courtisans of these times; 1631) depicts a bare-breasted
prostitute reading a letter as a old procuress holding
another note gestures to her. In the appended verses the
procuress speaks, "To this fresh vegetable only recently
arrived in this country, I secretly place a little letter in
her hand."

–PCS

Fig. 91. Crispijn van de Passe
Illustration from *Miroir des plus belles Courtisanes de ce temps,*
1631
Koninklijke Bibliotheek, The Hague

Cat. 33

169

PIETER DE HOOCH

(Rotterdam 1629–1684 Amsterdam)

The son of a master bricklayer and a midwife, Pieter Hendricks de Hooch (also spelled de Hoogh) was baptized in Rotterdam on December 20, 1629. According to Houbraken (1721), he was apprenticed to the Italianate landscapist Nicholaes Berchem, presumably in Haarlem, at the same time as his fellow Rotterdammer, the genre painter Jacob Ochtervelt. In 1652 de Hooch was in Delft, where he and the artist Hendrick van der Burch witnessed the signing of a will. The following year he was documented as a painter and servant (dienaar) to the linen merchant Justus de la Grange; an inventory of the latter's collection of thirty-six paintings drawn up in 1655 listed eleven by de Hooch. De Hooch was in Leiden in 1653 but living in Rotterdam in 1654, when he married Jannetje van der Burch, who in all likelihood was the sister of Hendrick. The couple had seven children. De Hooch joined the St. Luke's Guild in Delft in 1655 and paid dues in 1656 and 1657. His earliest dated paintings are of 1658, which show him to be already an accomplished master.

By April 1661 (and perhaps as much as eleven months earlier), he had settled in Amsterdam. Except for a visit to Delft in 1663, he seems to have remained in Amsterdam for the remainder of his life. The burial records of two of his children in 1663 and 1665 record that he was living on the Regulierspad and Engelspad respectively. These "paths" were located outside the old walls of the city and housed some of the poorest residents. By 1668 he had moved to the Konijnenstraat near the Lauriergracht. The majority of de Hooch's patrons seem to have been middle- and upper-class merchants, although in 1670 he portrayed the wealthy Jacott-Hoppesack family (Amsterdam Historical Museum). He never seems to have been wealthy enough to own a house, and his income was modest enough for him to escape the tax register of 1674. De Hooch baptized his last child in Amsterdam in 1672, and for the remaining dozen years of his life the only record we have of him is his paintings. A final document, referring to his burial in the Sint Anthonis Kerkhof in Amsterdam on March 24, 1684, states that he came from the *dolhuys* (bedlam); the date and circumstances of his entry into the insane asylum are unknown.

One of the most highly regarded seventeenth-century Dutch artists, Pieter de Hooch was a specialist in scenes of everyday life and portraits. Early in his career he executed guardroom scenes of soldiers taking their ease in stables or taverns or mustering out. While in Delft in the late 1650s he developed the highly distinctive style for which he is best remembered, depictions of middle-class interiors and sunny courtyards with perspective effects, an expressive use of light and space, a colorful palette, and silvery tonality. After he moved to Amsterdam his subjects became more elegant, his palette deeper, and his tonality darker. At the end of his career there was often a distressing decline in quality; whether this was related to his final illness is unknown. Although he influenced many artists, who are sometimes referred to inappropriately as the De Hooch School, he had no recorded pupils. Among the artists usually grouped with him are Hendrick van der Burch (his closest follower); Jacobus Vrel and Esaias Boursse (who are not known to have had any direct contact with him); Pieter Janssens Elinga; and the great Johannes Vermeer, with whom de Hooch undoubtedly became acquainted while in Delft.

–PCS

Literature: Hofstede de Groot, vol. 1 (1907); Valentiner 1930; Sutton 1980; exh. cat. Dulwich/Hartford 1998–99.

Cat. 34.
PIETER DE HOOCH
A Woman Reading a Letter by a Window, 1664
Signed and dated lower right on the crosspiece of the
table: *P.d.hoogh 1664*
Oil on canvas, 55 x 55 cm
Szépmüvészeti Múzeum, Budapest (Museum of Fine
Arts, Budapest), inv. no. 5933

Provenance: Possibly bought by P. J. Thys in Haarlem in
1800 and sold in July of that year to G. van der Pot van
Groeneveldt for 60 fl.; sale, G. van der Pot van
Groeneveldt, Rotterdam, June 6, 1808, to Allard of Paris,
155 fl.; Count Esterhazy, Papa, Hungary, c. 1850;
Countess Pálffy Pálmé, Budapest, by 1888; acquired by
the Museum of Fine Arts, Hungary, in 1923.

Exhibitions: Budapest 1888; Bordeaux, Galerie des
Beaux-Arts, *Trésors du Musée de Budapest*, 1972, no. 40;
Frankfurt 1993, no. 44, ill.

Literature: Hofstede de Groot, vol. 1 (1907), nos. 177
and 90; A. Pigler, *Katalog der Galerie alter Meister, Museum
der bildenden Künste*, vol. 1 (Budapest, 1968), p. 323, no.
5933, vol. 2, pl. 304; Sutton 1980, no. 63, pl. 67; exh. cat.,
Dulwich/Hartford 1998–99, p. 166, fig. 1.

Reading a letter that lies open on her lap, a woman
sits in shadow illuminated by a warm and atmospheric
light descending through an open window. She wears
an elegant light blue, fur-trimmed jacket, red skirt, and a
white apron. To her right is a straight-backed chair like
the one in which she sits, upholstered in leather with
diamond-shaped decorations, brass studs, and lion's-head
finials as appear frequently in interiors by de Hooch and
Vermeer. To her right in the shadows is a table covered
with an oriental carpet on which rests an open book.
Long curtains hang from the tall windows, and paintings
in black and gold frames grace the walls. The view
through the window, where the shutter has been thrown
open, offers a glimpse of rooftops and the tower of
Amsterdam's Westerkerk.

The dramatic contrasts of light and colored shadows,
the *contre-jour* lighting system, and the firm architectural
structure created by the large cross-shaped window are
typical of Pieter de Hooch's art after his move to
Amsterdam in about 1660–61. The work is dated 1664,
the only dated painting known by de Hooch from this
year and one of relatively few from the first decade of
his activity in Holland's largest and fastest-growing city.
Often smaller in format than the Delft period pictures
and the larger canvases from the 1670s, de Hooch's
works from the mid-1660s at times seem to imitate the
more intimate scale of Leiden School painting, which
had then become very popular and expensive. However,
he never achieved or attempted the level of refinement
in his brushwork that artists like Gerard Dou, Frans
van Mieris, or even Gabriel Metsu attained. Instead,
he sought a palette of more saturated hues and intense
effects of spotlit natural illumination.

The present painting, the artist's related work from
Stockholm (cat. 35), and other paintings by de Hooch
from the 1660s attest to his strong debt to Gerard ter
Borch, witnessed here in his choice of subject matter—
a woman quietly reading a letter—and evocation of a
more elegant setting than in de Hooch's Delft period
pictures. Ter Borch's purest treatment of the subject of
the lone female letter reader is the painting in the
Wallace Collection (Sutton essay, *fig. 7*); however, he also
depicted women taking a consoling drink as they read a
letter (cat. 10), or dressed in mourning black as they read
(*fig. 9*). More commonly he depicted women reading
letters in the company of others—confidants, servants,
messengers or delivery people (see, for example,
Gudlaugsson 1959–60, nos. 111, 142, 164, and 169).
However, ter Borch rarely makes the interior space of
his scenes an actively expressive component of his genre
scenes and never introduces an open window or glimpse
of the out-of-doors into his letter pictures. By contrast,
de Hooch invariably exploits the atmospheric effects of
his interiors and their subtle lighting effects, employing
openings and apertures to adjacent spaces and airy views
to the outside. These offer both an implicit reference
to the citizens of a wider world with whom the letter
reader communicates as well as a pleasing sense of
psychological release from the enclosed and neatly
circumscribed domestic world of women. Here the
poetic calm of the lone woman's still and rounded form
is enhanced by the shaft of light that enters the darkened
interior through the window, enlivening her intensely
focused concentration and seemingly conferring dramatic
import to the content of the missive.

–PCS

Cat. 35.
PIETER DE HOOCH
A Woman Reading a Letter with a Messenger by a Window
Oil on canvas, 57 x 49 cm
Nationalmuseum, Stockholm, inv. no. 471

Provenance: Queen Louisa Ulrica, Sweden, inv. 1760, no. 177; Royal Museum, inv. 1795, no. 205.

Exhibitions: Stockholm, Nationalmuseum, *Rembrandt och hans tid*, 1992–93, no. 123, ill.; Frankfurt 1993, no. 43; Dulwich/Hartford 1998–99, no. 35.

Literature: Hofstede de Groot, vol. 1 (1907), no. 198; Sutton 1980, pp. 37, 101, pl. 88, Ydema 1991, p. 184, no. 777.

In a high-ceilinged interior with a window at the left and a lighted doorway in the right distance, a woman in a red jacket and silver skirt with a small dog in her lap sits in the light reading a letter. Evidently an extended correspondence, the letter is composed of two sheets of paper. To the left is the messenger, wearing a bright blue jacket with red-orange cuffs, gold buttons down the front and around the sleeves, ample white linen, and a cravat. It is virtually the same costume worn by the messenger who delivers the letter to the young woman in the painting in Hamburg (*fig. 1*). He leans on the sill and gazes out the open window on the left. The glass of wine he holds in his hand no doubt is his refreshment, or *pourboire*, the gratuity extended to couriers. (Brekelenkam and others depicted couriers drinking while the recipient reads the letter; see Sutton essay, *fig. 31*) He waits, presumably to see if the lady would like him to deliver a response. To the right of the seated woman is a small table covered with an oriental carpet (of an unidentified variety, according to Ydema), a small stringed instrument, possibly a pochette, and an open music book, suggesting she had interrupted her playing to receive the letter. At the back and in the shadow is a serving woman who stands with hands clasped before her, looking toward her mistress with a sidelong gaze. Motionless and isolated, the still figures scarcely interact. Through the brilliantly lighted doorway in the right distance is a column suggesting that this elegant house has a grand portico or loggia, while in the lighted distance there is another substantial mansion with a carved pediment.

This painting probably postdates the related picture *Woman Reading a Letter* dated 1664 from Budapest (cat. 34), which also depicts the female reader seated in an elegant interior illuminated by the warm light of an open window and describes a similar hushed and still

Fig. 1. Pieter de Hooch
Messenger Delivering a Letter to a Young Woman
Oil on canvas, transferred from panel, 57 x 53 cm
Hamburger Kunsthalle, inv. no. 184

tone. The arrival of a letter once again breaks the daily routine, introducing a quiet interval of private communication that the attending servants observe with a respectful distance. The backlighted doorway, or *doorkijkje*, in the right distance is virtually de Hooch's signature motif. Here as elsewhere in his intimate art it offers a second and complementary light source to enrich the space of his shadowed interior while adding a pleasing sense of psychological release. Its august prospect also evokes an aristocratic world in which this lady presumably moves, a highborn, wealthy, and self-consciously literary sphere with rigorous epistolary conventions and etiquette. Ironically, de Hooch probably knew very little of this world he confects; he was the son of a bricklayer and midwife who seems to have lived very modestly in some of the poor sections of Amsterdam, dying in the madhouse.

–PCS

PIETER DE HOOCH

A Woman Directing a Young Man with a Letter, 1670
Signed and dated on the windowsill: *P. d'hooch. f. 1670*
Oil on canvas, 68 x 59 cm
Rijksmuseum, Amsterdam, inv. no. SK-C-147

Provenance: Madame Kemper, Leiden, 1827; J.
Meijnders, Amsterdam, 1838; A. van der Hoop,
Amsterdam, by 1842, who bequeathed it to the City in
1854.

Exhibitions: Amsterdam, Rijksmuseum, *Historische
Tentoonstelling der Stadt Amsterdam*, 1925, vol. 2, no. 421;
Schaffhausen, *Rembrandt und seine Zeit*, 1949, no. 62;
Capetown, National Gallery of South Africa, *Exhibition
of XVII Century Painting*, 1952, no. 24; Oslo,
Nasjongalleriet, *Fra Rembrandt ti Vermeer*, 1959, no. 33;
Brussels, Palais des Beaux-Arts, *Rembrandt en zijn tijd*,
1971, no. 56.

Literature: Smith, vol. 4 (1833), no. 51, *Supplement*
(1844), no. 22; W. Thoré-Bürger, *Les Musées de la
Hollande*, vol. 2 (Paris, 1860), pp. 58–59; Hofstede de
Groot, vol. 1 (1907), no. 173; Sutton 1980, no. 94, pl. 96;
Sutton, in exh. cat. Dulwich/Hartford 1998–99, pp. 40,
58–60, figs. 33a, 58.

In the front room of a house on a canal, a woman in
an ice blue jacket, ocher-orange skirt, and pearl earrings
sits in a chair on a *soldertje* (little platform) by the light of
the window. She has a small lapdog in her lap and holds
an open letter in her right hand while gesturing to an
adolescent boy who stands at the right, who apparently
has just come through a doorway at the right. Holding
up a second letter in his right hand and his hat in his
left, he steps to the left toward the open door. Filling the
shadowed foreground with soft illumination, the lighted
doorway and the tall windows in the front of the house
offer a view of trees, a relatively wide canal, and the
brilliantly lit facades of elegant town houses on the
sunny side in the distance. A brown, tan, and white
beagle ambles across the elegant marble floor, while
through the door a small child appears in an elaborate
dress and beribboned hat holding a small whip for
spinning a toy top. Two men appear before the house
in the distance on the far side of the canal. Cornelis
Hofstede de Groot (1907) identified the canal as the
Kloveniersburgwal in Amsterdam.

Dated 1670, thus painted about nine years after
Pieter de Hooch had moved from Delft to the booming
metropolis of Amsterdam, this is a mature work from the
artist's later career. It demonstrates that he was still fully

in expressive command of perspective and his
preternatural ability to capture subtle effects of daylight,
in this case juxtaposing the darkened foreground, cast in
shadow by the canyon of one of Amsterdam's grander
canals, and the lighted distance. (The single-point
perspective was created by placing a pin at the vanishing
point from which the lines of the orthogonals were
drawn; the pinhole is still visible in the facade of the
building viewed through the window.) After moving
to Amsterdam, de Hooch began to depict more elegant
and grander homes in which the presiding mistress
approximated the ideal described in contemporary
domestic conduct manuals by Jacob Cats and other
authors. An ideal, she became the administrator of a well-
run, prosperous household with rich furnishings, a well-
provisioned kitchen, contented family, and well-behaved
servants. In the present painting the fashionably tailored
lady seated beneath the window is probably the mother
of the extravagantly dressed child (possibly a boy,
notwithstanding the dress) and undoubtedly the mistress
and manager of the household. She has received a letter
that lies open in her lap but seems to direct the young
man at the right to deliver a second letter. This young
man is probably a member of the household, possibly
her son but more likely a servant or apprentice. Unlike
in larger cities, such as London, Paris, and Vienna,
Amsterdam had no internal municipal postal service;
letters were carried between citizens and across the
manageably-sized town by servants, family members,
or private couriers.

In the present work, the comforting geometry, the
penumbra of the front room, and the spare and laconic
gestures that set the everyday narrative and missive on
their way evoke a measured domestic world that utterly
charmed that nineteenth-century champion of the
heroism of the quotidian, W. Thoré-Bürger. Thoré-Bürger
regularly likened the descriptive veracity of Dutch genre
paintings to the writings of George Sand and Gustave
Flaubert. Enthusing over the present work, he compared
it to the novels of Honoré de Balzac, in which the
minute description of the setting and the characters seem
to foretell the narrative. He wrote in 1860, "Balzac's
preceding topography is useful in understanding de
Hooch's paintings, in which the domestic interior—the
home as the English call it—with all its charms, has such
importance. It isn't that the people there are accessories,
but they are inseparable from the [place]. Everything is
created for them, above all the light that animates and
cheers them. All is a harmonious milieu, where one can
live as in one's own home, doing something, nothing
much, perhaps nothing at all."

–PCS

Cat. 37.
PIETER DE HOOCH
Man Reading a Letter to a Woman
Signed on the foot warmer: *P.d.Hoo…*
Oil on canvas, 77 x 69.9 cm
Fondation Aetas Aurea, cat. no. 17

Provevnance: William Joseph, baron van Brienen, heer van de Groote Lindt Dortsmond, Stad aan het Haringvliet and Wassenaar (1760–1839), 182 Herengracht, Amsterdam, 1811–13; his son Arnold Willem, baron van Brienen, heer van de Groote Lindt Dortsmond, Stad aan het Haringvliet and Wassenaar, chamberlain to the king of the Netherlands, his sale, Paris, May 8, 1865, no. 15 (unsold); by descent to private collection, Paris; sale, Christie's, London, July 4, 1997, no. 19.

Exhibitions: Dulwich/Hartford 1998–99, no. 39, ill.; Osaka 2000, no. 24.

Literature: Hofstede de Groot, vol. 1 (1907), no. 240; Sutton 1980, pp. 37, 44, 104–5, cat. 97, pl. 101; exh. cat. Frankfurt 1993, p. 224, no. 4; Marcel Roethlisberger, *Abraham van Bloemaert and His Sons* (Doornspijk, 1993), p. 252, no. 5; P. van der Ploeg, E. Runia, and A. van Suchtelen, *Dutch and Flemish Old Masters from the Kremer Collection* (The Hague, 2002), pp. 84–87, no. 17, ill.

A seated man in a brown coat with purple cuffs and ribbons at his shoulders wears a broad-brimmed black hat with silver trim. He places one hand on his knee and holds in the other a multipaged letter or similar pieces of paper with writing and seems to read aloud to the woman seated beside him. Wearing a bright red coat and shoes, gold skirt, white apron, and pearl earrings, she has interrupted her needlework and inclines her head as if listening. Her sewing basket rests on the floor beside her. The light descends diagonally from an unseen window at the left and illuminates the letter as well as a desk to the left on which lie another sheet of paper and a small book. The comfortable room has an elegant black-and-white marble floor, tiled wainscoting, a beamed ceiling, and a tall hearth with a *rabat* (a cloth valance hanging down from the hearth). In the shadow of the hearth there appears to be a box stove. On the floor at the lower left is a small foot warmer. On the back wall hangs a crepuscular landscape in a gold frame and over the mantel a nocturnal scene of the Nativity. De Hooch often based the paintings within his paintings on prints, in this case on Cornelis Bloemaert's engraving of 1625 after Abraham Bloemaert's painting of this subject in the Herzog Anton Ulrich-Museum in Braunschweig. The

Latin inscription on the print expressed Christ's message of piety and humility: "Descended from heaven, miraculous incarnation of the Father. He assumes the frail fabric of the human flesh. As the very God, you are lying in the stable on hard straw, seeking and teaching poverty."

Other artists, such as Ludolph de Jongh and Adriaen van Ostade (see Sutton essay, *figs. 19 & 16*), depicted figures reading letters and broadsheets aloud, but usually to a crowd of peasants or simple folk gathered in a tavern. In those works the suggestion is that the listeners might be illiterate. In the well-furnished and prosperous home depicted here it is less likely that the woman could not read herself, although women had lower literacy rates than men in the seventeenth century. It is more probable that the man wants to share the contents of the letter, its news and artistry, aloud. As noted in the Introduction to this catalogue, letter-writing manuals stressed that letters should be the written equivalent of polite conversation and that the exchange of letters were the enduring representation of spoken dialogue. It follows that well-written letters were well suited to be read aloud. As Jean Puget de la Serre and Paul Jacob explained in the prefaces to their manuals, the letter's purpose was to enter the reader's thoughts and imagination and persuade them of the message, be it a business proposal or a love letter. The woman's self-forgetful expression of reverie here seems to embody the goal of a well-written letter. Whether the small volume on the table is a letter-writing manual is unknowable, but in the present context the possibility exists.

–PCS

JOHANNES VERMEER

(Delft 1632–1675 Delft)

Born in Delft in 1632, Johannes Vermeer was the son of Reynier Jansz. (Vos), whose professions were described as weaver, innkeeper (he rented De Vliegende Vos, The Flying Fox, in Delft from 1627 to 1630), and master art dealer. His mother was Digna Baltens. The couple bought a house and adjoining inn called Mechelen on the Groote Markt in Delft in 1641. Vermeer's teacher is not known but may have been the local history painter Leonart Bramer (1596–1674), who was a witness to the posting of Vermeer's wedding banns to Catharina Bolnes (b. 1631) in Delft in 1653. She was the daughter of Reynier Bolnes and Maria Thins, who had separated. Vermeer must have converted to Catholicism before his wedding into a family of that faith in April 1653. In the same month Vermeer signed a document with Gerard ter Borch in Delft and in December registered in the St. Luke's Guild as a master painter. His early paintings suggest contact with the Utrecht Caravaggisti but he soon began painting smaller interior genre scenes with expressive use of light, space, and perspective in the manner of Pieter de Hooch, who also was active in Delft and three years his senior. In 1656 he paid fees to the guild and dated the earlier of his only two dated works, *The Procuress* (Gemäldegalerie, Dresden). In 1657 he and his wife borrowed two hundred florins from a wealthy burgher, Pieter Claesz. van Ruijven. John Michael Montias has discovered a great deal of circumstantial evidence suggesting that van Ruijven was Vermeer's primary patron, including the inventory drawn up of the possessions of van Ruijven's daughter in 1683, which included no fewer than twenty paintings by Vermeer, which undoubtedly were inherited from her parents. Gerard Dou and Frans van Mieris are known to have worked for similar faithful patrons. Vermeer was named as a beneficiary in his mother-in-law's will in 1657. Thereafter she contributed significantly to the support of her daughter and son-in-law and their children, who from at least 1660 on lived in Maria Thins's house in the Papists' corner in Delft. In 1662 he was named *hoofdman* (headman) of the guild for two years and again in 1670. As evidence of his growing reputation, Vermeer was visited by the French diplomat Balthasar de Moncony in Delft in 1663, and in 1667 he was praised as the artistic successor to Carel Fabritius in a poem by Arnold Bon, published in Dirck van Bleyswijck's chronicle of the city of Delft. In 1669 Pieter Teding van Berckhout, a prominent citizen of The Hague, visited Vermeer twice. Following the death of his mother and sister in the previous year, Vermeer inherited the house Mechelen in 1670. He leased out the latter in 1672. The same year, together with other artists, Vermeer was called to The Hague to judge a group of Italian paintings. In 1674 Vermeer traveled to Gouda on behalf of Maria Thins to settle the estate of his deceased father-in-law. The following year he went to Amsterdam, once again on her behalf, and while there borrowed one thousand guilders. When he died that December, at age forty-three, he was deeply in debt. Vermeer was buried in the Oude Kerk in Delft. He was survived by Catharina and eleven children, ten of them minors. Following his death, his widow was forced to sell two paintings (see cat. 39) to a baker to cover her costs for bread and tried to settle other debts with paintings. In 1676 she petitioned the high court to issue letters of cession to her creditors, citing the disastrous conditions caused by the war with France and her husband's death. The great scientist and perfector of the microscope, Anthony van Leeuwenhoek, was appointed the executor of Vermeer's estate and in that capacity tried mightily to settle the late painter's debts. He sought, for example, to wrest Vermeer's own *Art of Painting* (Kunsthistorisches Museum, Vienna) from Maria Thins, who claimed it as partial settlement of her daughter's debts to her, evidently to keep the artist's magnum opus in the family.

Vermeer was active primarily as a painter of genre scenes, but he also produced masterful works in other subject categories, including history paintings, townscapes (*The View of Delft*, Maurithuis, The Hague), and *tronijen* (*The Girl with the Pearl Earring*, also in the Mauritshuis). He evidently worked very carefully and slowly; only about thirty-four works survive today and, judging from the paucity of early sales references, his original oeuvre is unlikely to have been substantially larger. The scarcity of his paintings probably explains why so little was known of his art when he was "rediscovered" by W. Thoré-Bürger in 1866. Yet today he is the most celebrated of all Dutch genre painters.

–PCS

Literature: Thoré-Bürger 1866; Hofstede de Groot, vol. 1 (1907), pp. 579–607; A. B. de Vries, *Johannes Vermeer van Delft*, 2d ed. (London, 1948); P. T. A. Swillens, Johannes *Vermeer: Painter of Delft* (Brussels, 1950); Gowing 1952; Albert Blankert, *Johannes Vermeer van Delft (1632–1675)* (Utrecht, 1975); Blankert 1978; Wheelock 1981; Montias 1987; Montias 1989; exh. cat. Washington/The Hague 1995–96; Gaskell and Joncker 1998; exh. cat. New York/London 2001; Franits 2001.

with the present work, such as the broom and slippers. The Louvre painting has been cited (see Wadum, in Gaskell and Joncker 1998, p. 204) as a possible source for Vermeer's *Woman Asleep* (The Metropolitan Museum of Art, New York), which undoubtedly predates the present work and is the master's only other surviving painting to use a *doorkijkje*, or view to an adjoining space. (A painting in the Dissius sale in 1696 was described as depicting "a gentleman washing his hands in a see-through room with sculpture.") This device is more commonly and rightly associated with Pieter de Hooch (see, for example, cat. 36), who probably influenced the younger Vermeer when they were together in Delft. De Hooch's *Couple with a Parrot* (Wallraf-Richartz-Museum, Cologne) employs a composition very similar to that of *The Love Letter*. Indeed, the two paintings must be related, indicating that the artists remained in contact even after de Hooch moved to Amsterdam. The de Hooch has been mistakenly assumed to be dated 1668 (see Washington/The Hague 1995–96, p. 180), but it is in fact undated (see Dulwich/Hartford 1998–99, cat. 40, ill.) and may have been executed after the present work, suggesting that the direction of influence between the two colleagues may have been reversed later in their careers. The authors of the Vermeer exhibition catalogue (see Washington/The Hague 1995–96, p. 182) observed in connection with the present work that Pieter Teding van Berckhout, who visited Vermeer in 1669, observed, "the most extraordinary and curious aspect [of his art] is in the perspective." They also suggested that the visual contrast between the darkened and somewhat unkempt foreground and the tidier lighted distance (a juxtaposition that they found "unsettling") may have a bearing on the painting's expressive message.

–PCS

Fig. 1. Samuel van Hoogstraten *Perspective through a Doorway*, 1658 Oil on canvas, 103 x 70 cm Musée du Louvre, Paris, inv. no. RF 3722

Cat. 39.
JOHANNES VERMEER
Lady Writing a Letter with her Maidservant
Signed on the paper hanging over the table edge: *IVMeer* (the first three letters in ligature)
Oil on canvas, 72.2 x 59.7 cm
National Gallery of Ireland, Dublin, cat. no. 4535

Provenance: Catharina Bolnes, widow of Vermeer, Delft, 1676; Hendrick van Buyten, Delft, 1676–1701; Josua van Belle, Rotterdam, before 1710; Ida Catharina van der Meyden, widow of van Belle, Rotterdam, 1710–29; sale, van Belle, Rotterdam, September 6, 1730, no. 92 (155 fl.); Franco van Bleyswijk, Delft, 1734; Catharina van der Burch, married to Hendrick van Slingelandt, The Hague, 1761–75; possibly Barthout van Slingelandt, Dordrecht, 1771–98; Viktor von Miller zu Aichholz, Vienna, before 1881; with Charles Sedelmeyer, Paris, 1881, sold to Secrétan; Secrétan, Paris, 1881–89; sale, Secrétan, Paris, June 1, 1889, no. 140 (62,000 francs to Boussod, Valadon & Cie.); Marinoni Collection, Paris; with F. Kleinberger, Paris; Alfred Beit, London, c. 1895–1906; Sir Otto Beit Bt, London, 1906–30; Sir Alfred Beit, 2d Bt, London and (from 1952) Blessington, Russborough, near Dublin (1930–86, when the painting was stolen); The National Gallery of Ireland, gifted by Beit in 1987; the painting recovered in 1993.

Exhibitions: Washington/The Hague 1995–96, no. 19 (with a list of all earlier exhs. and lit.); Amsterdam 2000

Literature: Thoré-Bürger 1866, p. 548; Hofstede de Groot, vol. 1 (1907), no. 35; Gowing 1952; Blankert 1978, pp. 35, 56, 168–69, no. 27, pls. 27 and 27a; Wheelock 1981, pp. 33, 134, 146, 150, pl. 27; Montias 1987, p. 75 n. 54; Montias 1989, p. 266 and ill.; Wheelock 1995, pp. 5, 6, 7, 31, 156–62, 184, ill. 107; Blankert, in exh. cat. Washington/The Hague 1995–96, p. 39; Lisa Vergara, "*Antiek* and *Modern* in Vermeer's *Lady Writing a Letter with Her Maid*," in Gaskell and Joncker 1998, pp. 235–49, ills.; Liedtke, in exh. cat. New York/London 2001, p. 168, fig. 178.

In the corner of a room illuminated by a tall window in the left wall a woman in a pale green dress with white cap and sleeves and pearl earrings sits at a table covered with an oriental carpet writing a letter. Behind her and to the left stands a maidservant in a more subdued tan and gray outfit with a blue apron. A calm and columnar figure, she crosses her arms and waits while gazing sidelong out the window. Her mistress, in contrast, sets earnestly to her task. The elegant interior features a dark green curtain on the left, black and white marble floor

with a skirt of tiles, and a large painting of the Finding of Moses (attributed by some to Peter Lely, who was trained in Haarlem) in an ebony frame on the back wall. A translucent lace curtain hangs down from the leaded glass window. The pattern and diffusion of light are carefully distributed by closing the lower exterior shutter on the right. As elsewhere in Vermeer's art (see cat. 38), the geometry of the painting is carefully calculated to underpin and portion out the space clearly. For example, the edge of the table is the same distance from the bottom of the picture as the bottom of the ebony frame is from the top. In creating his perspective, Vermeer has also chosen a relatively low viewing point, scarcely higher than the top of the table, which adds to the figures' monumentality and enhances the height of the space.

One small detail that animates the scene and has a potential bearing on its meaning is the small still life on the floor at the lower right corner (see detail). It includes a letter, a stick of sealing wax, a bright red seal, and an

object that has been interpreted either as a small book (Blankert) or "a letter [with] its wrapper crumpled" (Vergara). The latter's suggestion is that this is either a letter that the lady has received or a discarded draft of a letter, to which she returns so single-mindedly. As has been suggested in the Sutton essay, letters were sometimes enclosed in cloth or paper envelopes in the seventeenth century, but usually were simply folded, sealed with wax, and addressed, and sometimes secured with twine. In either case, the fact that the letter and postal instruments have been cast to the floor implies a state of some agitation that belies the calm atmosphere of the interior. Blankert (in exh. cat. Washington/The Hague, 1995–96) suggested that the object might be a book, specifically one of the fashionable small letter-writing manuals that writers often consulted during composition (see Sutton essay). In that case, it would imply that the lady had found no prescription in the book for the letter she now writes and chose to compose it in her own words and with her own

Cat. 39, detail

emotions. Though offering exemplary love letters with varying degrees of demure decorum and ardor, letter manuals increasingly claimed no ideal form or style for love letters, which were regarded as uniquely individual to their author and their intended.

We also note that the empty chair on the near side of the table here suggests that someone has recently been sitting there, since chairs of this type (which were not upholstered on the back) were not left freestanding in rooms of this period but placed against the wall when not in use (see cat. 40). Had the objects not been tossed to the floor and the chair not been in use recently, the very correct-looking maidservant surely would have tidied them up. Thus by implication the viewer is complicit in this private drama, an idea that goes to the essence of epistolary literature.

The depiction of the Finding of Moses undoubtedly also has a bearing on the painting's subject and has been discussed, though its meaning remains obscure. The same painting appears on a smaller scale in the background of Vermeer's *Astronomer*, dated 1668 (Musée du Louvre, Paris), and, like other paintings within Vermeer's paintings, may have been owned by his family (see discussion of cat. 38). The subject naturally appealed on one level because it depicted ladies bathing, and on a more elevated plane as a biblical tale. The Old Testament story of Moses, expanded by Flavius Josephus in his widely read *Jewish Antiquities*, was well known and revered by the Dutch, who illustrated many episodes from the life of the prophet in history paintings, but none so frequently as the Finding of Moses. The story (Exod. 2:1–10) recounts how Moses' mother hid her son in a basket to save him from Pharaoh's decree that all male Hebrew infants be executed. Pharaoh's daughter, called Thermuthis by Josephus and celebrated in seventeenth-century Dutch literature as a paragon of beauty and compassion, found the child, raised him, and called him Moses. As Wheelock first observed (see 1981, and exh. cat. Washington/The Hague 1995–96), the popular story was interpreted in the seventeenth century as evidence of Divine Providence and God's ability to bring together opposing factions. Thus the associations of the painting within the painting could be connected with the letter writer by their shared good intentions of salvation (wishes for the care and health of the author's intended) and reconciliation, which brings about the serenity here embodied in the domestic setting by following God's divine plan.

Vergara (1998) related the painting to Gerard de Lairesse's art theory of the *Antiek* and the *Modern* in his *Groot Schilderboek* (Amsterdam 1707, pt. 1, bk. 3). In his theory, albeit published after Vermeer's death, he distinguished the "Antique" subjects as embodying all that is noble, ancient, and enduring, while the "Modern," which approximates what we now call "genre," encompasses all that is secular, domestic, quotidian, and ephemeral (see discussion in Sutton essay). While Lairesse preferred and extolled the former, he allowed that many sentiments could be expressed in both modes, and that the modern mode, especially when depicting elegant upper-class subjects, offered artists greater personal freedom. In Vergara's view, Vermeer was stating his own ambitions for modern painting by combining the biblical and the haute bourgeoisie, thus placing the letter writer in the tradition of ideal femininity embodied by Pharaoh's daughter.

Vermeer never sold this painting in his lifetime. At his death it remained with his widow, Catharina Bolnes, who was forced to give it with another painting as security to a baker and art collector, Hendrick van Buyten, to whom she owed the sizable sum of 617 guilders for bread. The painting eventually was acquired by the fabulously wealthy collector Alfred Beit (1853–1906), who made his fortunes in South African diamond and gold mines. It descended to his nephew, also called Alfred (1903–1994), who acquired the Palladian country house Russborough, in Blessington, near Dublin. From there it was stolen twice, first by the IRA in 1974 and a second time in 1986 by the Dublin underworld, but was recovered in 1993, in time for Sir Alfred to see its rescue and installation in the National Gallery of Ireland, to which he had gifted this painting and his Metsus (see cats. 18 & 19) in 1987.

–PCS

PIETER JANSSENS ELINGA

(Bruges 1623–before 1682 Amsterdam)

Born on August 18, 1623, Pieter Janssens Elinga was the son of a painter in Bruges, Flanders. Although he probably first studied with his father, Gijsbrecht Janssens, his name does not appear in the register of the local painters' guild. Following the death of his first wife, Beatrix van der Mijlen, an inventory was drawn up of Janssens Elinga's possessions in Rotterdam on August 22, 1653. The inventory was ordered by the Chamber of Orphans to protect the interests of the couple's child, indicating that the artist had financial difficulties. Janssens Elinga subsequently moved to Amsterdam, where a person of his name but whose profession was given as musician became a citizen on March 16, 1657. An inventory of the possessions of Anthonie Pannekoeck of Amsterdam included a *vanitas* painting by Janssens Elinga in 1661. By September 1662 the artist-actor Janssens Elinga and his second wife, Jurina Bos, were living on the Breestraat, the street where Rembrandt had lived until 1658. The couple had four children. Jurina was listed as a widow on September 24, 1682.

Janssens Elinga was active as a painter of both interior genre scenes with perspective effects and still lifes. The former are clearly influenced by the art of Pieter de Hooch (q.v.) and in the eighteenth and nineteenth centuries were often misattributed to him. However, there is no evidence to suggest that Janssens Elinga or any other artist was de Hooch's pupil.

—PCS

Literature: Cornelis Hofstede de Groot, "Johannes Janssens," *Zeitschrift für bildende Kunst*, n.s., 1 (1890), pp. 132–35; Cornelis Hofstede de Groot, "De schilder Janssens [Elinga], een navolger van Pieter de Hooch," *Oud Holland* 9 (1891), pp. 266–96; Brière-Misme 1947–48; exh. cat. Philadelphia/Berlin/London 1984, pp. 202–3.

Cat. 40.
PIETER JANSSENS ELINGA
A Woman Reading a Letter and a Woman Sweeping
Oil on canvas, 83.4 x 100.2 cm
Städelsches Kunstinstitut, Frankfurt am Main, inv. no. 1129

Provenance: Sale, Paulus van Romondt of Kampen, Amsterdam, May 14, 1835, no. 11 (as Jansen van Keulen), to de Gruyter; sale, Jean-Jacques-Marie Meffre, comte de Morny, Paris, February 26, 1845, no. 43 (as Pieter de Hooch, 5,900 francs); sale, Charles Piérard of Valenciennes, Escribe, Paris, March 20–21, 1860, no. 28 (as Pieter de Hooch, to Blanc, 20,200 francs); sale, Madame Blanc, Paris, May 3, 1876, no. 13 (as Pieter de Hooch), with an etching by Lalauze, to dealer Bourgeois of Cologne; acquired from Bourgeois for the Städelsches Kunstinstitut by the Frankfurter Kunstverein (as Pieter de Hooch, 42,750 marks).

Literature: Levin, "Eine gefälsche Gemälde Galerie," *Kunstchronik*, 1887, p. 677; idem, "Noch ein Wort in Sachen des Städelschen Instituts," *Kunstchronik*, 1888, p. 256; Cornelis Hofstede de Groot, "Johannes Janssens," *Zeitschrift für bildende Kunst*, n.s., 1 (1890), pp. 134–35 (as Janssens Elinga); C. Hofstede de Groot, "De schilder Janssens, een navolger van Pieter de Hooch," *Oud Holland* 9 (1891), pp. 284–85, no. 7; Hofstede de Groot, vol. 1 (1907), p. 569, no. 12 (under works falsely attributed to Pieter de Hooch); Brière-Misme 1947–48, pp. 90–91, fig. 1, pp. 166–68 n. 7; exh. cat. Philadelphia/Berlin/London 1984, p. 203 nn. 6–7; Jochen Sander, *Niederländische Gemälde vor 1800 in bedeutenden Sammlungen, Städel, Frankfurt am Main* (Frankfurt, 1995), p. 37, pl. 76.

At the back of a tall, shadowed interior into which a bright shaft of light falls, a woman sits reading a letter as a maidservant sweeps the floor in the foreground. The lady wears a bright yellow and red top with a light green skirt, mauve overskirt, and white headdress. The maidservant is more modestly dressed in a brown skirt, black top, white apron, and red cuffs. Through an open door at the back left one glimpses a second backlit room, where a man wearing a long coat, red cuffs, yellow stockings, and bushy hair stands before a table and chair both covered in blue fabric. Both lateral walls are visible in the room in the foreground, which is illuminated by tall half-shuttered windows with red curtains in the back wall. A mirror in a gold frame hangs between the two tall windows. The patterned floor is of marble and framed landscapes decorate the walls. Three chairs are set against the walls. A shaft of sunlight casts a dramatic shadow on

190

signed and dated 1680, present location unknown (see exh. cat. Worcester Art Museum, *17th Century Dutch Art*, 1979, fig. 15b). The *Lady at Her Dressing Table* that was attributed to Frans van Mieris when exhibited at the Worcester Art Museum in 1979 (their no. 15) was sold as a Jan van Mieris in the nineteenth century and may also be by Frans's son Jan.

The conjunction between the letter theme and the game of tric-trac occurs elsewhere in Dutch genre painting (see cat. 42) and seems to underscore the fact that letters can bring news that precipitate dramatic changes in people's lives. The game of tric-trac is called *verkeerspel* in Dutch and literally means "game of changes." In sixteenth- and seventeenth-century art, tric-trac was an attribute of personifications of idleness (see the woodcut *Luiheid* by Cornelis Anthonisz.) and often figured in moralizing print series by Jacob Matham and others condemning the idle pastimes of drunks and tavern dwellers (see E. de Jongh et al., in exh. cat. Amsterdam 1976, under no. 22). While nothing in the elegant tone of the present work suggests that the game's negative associations were uppermost in the artist's mind, the slight smile that crosses the face of the woman reader suggests that life's changes have gone in her favor with the receipt of this letter. The present work undoubtedly depicts a fictitious scene but one calculated to evoke the height of fashion in about 1680. The housecoat and fur cap that the man wears is a style that appears elsewhere in high-style genre, notably in the works of the Delft painter Cornelis de Man (see *Man Giving a Letter to a Maidservant*, Musée des Beaux-Arts, Marseilles) who also favored similar furniture. These housecoats seem to have been inspired by the padded silk kimonos presented by the shogun to delegates of the Dutch India Company and which subsequently became the height of prestige and fashion (see cat. 24).

–PCS

NICOLAES VERKOLJE
(Delft 1673–1746 Amsterdam)

Nicolaes Verkolje was born on April 11, 1673, the son of the Delft painter Johannes Verkolje (q.v.), with whom he studied. In 1700 Nicolaes moved to Amsterdam, where he remained until his death on January 21, 1746. In addition to genre scenes, he painted mythological subjects, decorative murals and ceilings, and portraits. He often modeled his work after examples by seventeenth-century genre painters, above all those by Gerard Dou and the Leiden *fijnschilders*, but also Gabriel Metsu, Gerard ter Borch, and Adriaen van der Werff.

Cat. 44.
NICOLAES VERKOLJE
Young Woman with a Candle and a Letter in a Window with a Maidservant
Oil on panel, 33.7 x 27.6 cm
The Menil Collection, Houston. Gift of Baroness Tamara de Kuffner de Lempicka, inv. no. 67-30

Provenance: Sale, Heineken et al., Paris, February 13–18, 1758, no. 65; Baroness Tamara de Kuffner de Lempicka.

Literature: C. J. A. Wansink, "Een terruggevonden schilderij van Nicolaas Verkolje," *Oud Holland* 101 (1987), pp. 86–88, fig. 1.

Engraved: Jean-Baptiste Michel.

In a nocturnal scene, a young woman leans out a window with a blazing candle in a candlestick holder in her right hand and a letter raised in her left. She smiles as she looks down at someone unseen; she wears a blue-and-white striped gown with open bodice featuring an ample décolleté. Behind her a grinning maidservant with headdress and kerchief points a finger to her nose in a significant gesture. To either side of the window in the darkness are brick-red shutters and below it, to the right, a facade stone (*gevelsteen*), inscribed, "'t land van b . . ." and depicting a partially visible man carrying a large bunch of grapes.

This painting was long without a firm attribution until the connoisseurs at the Rijksbureau voor Kunsthistorishes Documentatie in The Hague recognized it as the work of Nicolaes Verkolje, the son of Johannes Verkolje (q.v.), an accomplished later practitioner of the

Fig. 1. Nicolaes Verkolje
*Young Man and a Young Woman
with a Rose*
Oil on panel, 38 x 31 cm
Národní Galerie, Prague,
inv. no. DO-4568

Fig. 2. Gerard Dou
*Young Woman with a lighted Candle
at a Window,* c. 1658–65
Signed
Oil on panel, 26.5 x 19.5 cm
Museo Thyssen-Bornemisza.
Madrid, cat. 132

Leiden *fijnschilder* manner. With its open-window, aperture design enhancing the illusion of space, its smooth execution, and pastel palette, the painting may be compared with another work by Nicolaes Verkolje, *Young Man and a Young Woman with a Rose* in the museum in Prague (*fig. 1*). The inspiration for this type of highly finished, nocturnal, window or "niche" scene was the paintings produced about a half century earlier in Leiden by Gerard Dou. As C. J. A. Wansink observed in an article devoted to the present painting (1987), Dou executed a very similar nocturnal, half-length painting of a smiling young woman holding a lighted candle in a window which probably was the inspiration for the present work; the Dou was in an Amsterdam collection in Verkolje's day and is now preserved in the Thyssen-Bornemisza Collection, Madrid (*fig. 2*).

The subject of the painting probably involves the young woman's encouragements to the unseen suitor. In a reproductive print of the present work produced in the eighteenth century by Jean-Baptiste Michel, the painting was entitled *La Belle Impatiënte* (The Beautiful Impatient One). And as Wansink (1987) has observed, a lost drawing after the work by the eighteenth-century artist Jan Stolker, which was described in detail in a sale catalogue in 1786, pointed out the maidservant's gesture as underscoring the fact that the young woman is receptive to the unseen young man's advances: "achter haar staat een Meid, welke met den voorvinger de neus te houden, als 't ware te kennen geeft, haar Juffrouw te willen verrassen, door haar dien blaker te willen ontneemen" (behind her stands a maid who holds her forefinger to her nose to intimate the truth of the matter

that her mistress wishes to emphasize through the candlestick that she is receptive to him). As Wansink again observed, the fragmentary image and cropped text on the facade stone probably refers to the fortunate vineyard workers in the land of Canaan, known as "'t Land van Belofte" (the Promised Land [of the Israelites]), and traditionally understood to refer to the afterlife. The theme commonly figured on the decorations of facade stones in Amsterdam where Verkolje lived and worked (see H. W. Alings, *Amsterdamsche gevelstenen* [Amsterdam, 1943], p. 34).

It is conceivable that one could interpret the lady's inviting gesture as the promise implicit in the *gevelsteen*, but it is more likely that the facade stone offers a moral contrast and admonition. The grapes of Canaan traditionally symbolized Christ, whose blood (embodied in the wine of the Eucharist) forgave man for the First Fall and Original Sin and made possible access to the Promised Land of the afterlife. Given the probability that some of Verkolje's other genre scenes, including the picture now in Prague (*fig. 1*; see L. Slavíèek, in *Umení* 34, no. 2 [1986], pp. 151–57), seem to encode moral messages, it is possible that the present work also embodies an admonition. Wansink plausibly suggests that it should be interpreted as a warning to the unseen suitor to consider that accepting the young lady's tempting offer may jeopardize the more permanent rewards of the promised afterlife. With a point of view outside and below the midpoint of the picture plane but in the vicinity of the supposed suitor, we as viewers may also consider ourselves recipients of the artist's admonition.

–PCS

Bibliography

Literature

Alpers 1983
Svetlana Alpers. *The Art of Describing: Dutch Art in the Seventeenth Century*. Chicago, 1983.

Angel 1642
Philips Angel. *Lof der schilderconst*. Leiden, 1642.

Bernt 1970
Walther Bernt. *The Netherlandish Painters of the Seventeenth Century*. 3 vols. London, 1970.

Bille 1961
Clara Bille. *De temple der kunst of het kabinet van den Heer Braamcamp*. 2 vols. Amsterdam, 1961.

Blankert 1978
Albert Blankert. *Vermeer of Delft: Complete Edition of the Paintings*. Oxford, 1978.

Bode 1883
Wilhelm von Bode. *Studien zur Geschichte der holländischen Malerei*. Braunschweig, 1883.

Braun 1980
Karel Braun. *Alle tot nu toe bekende schilderijen van Jan Steen*. Rotterdam, 1980.

Bredius 1927
Abraham Bredius. *Jan Steen*. Amsterdam, 1927.

Brière-Misme 1947–48
Clothide Brière-Misme. "A Dutch Intimist, Pieter Janssens Elinga." Parts 1–4. *Gazette des Beaux-Arts* 6th ser., 31 (1947), pp. 89–102, 113–64; 32 (1947), pp. 159–76; 33 (1948), pp. 347–66.

Broos 1987
B. P. J. Broos. *Meesterwerken in het Mauritshuis*. The Hague, 1987.

Cats 1665
Jacob Cats. *Alle de Wercken. Proefsteen van den Trouringh*. Amsterdam, 1665.

Van Deursen 1991
A. Th. Van Deursen. *Plain Lives in a Golden Age: Popular Culture, Religion and Society in Seventeenth Century Holland*. Translated by Maarten Ultee. Cambridge, 1991.

Franits 1997
Wayne Franits, ed. *Looking at Seventeeth-Century Dutch Art: Realism Reconsidered*. Cambridge, 1997.

Franits 2001
Wayne Franits, ed. *The Cambridge Companion to Vermeer*. Cambridge, 2001.

Gaskell and Joncker 1998
Ivan Gaskell and Michiel Joncker, eds. *Vermeer Studies*. Studies in the History of the Visual Arts, Symposium Papers 33. Washington, D.C., 1998.

Gowing 1952
Lawrence Gowing. *VermeerI*. London, 1952.
Gudlaugsson 1959–60

S. J. Gudlaugsson. *Gerard ter Borch*. 2 vols. The Hague, 1959–60.

Gudlaugsson 1968
———. "Kantekeningen bij de ontwikkeling van Metsu." *Oud Holland* 83 (1968), pp. 13–44.

de Groot 1952
Cornelis Wilhelmus de Groot. *Jan Steen. Beeld en woord*. Utrecht, 1952.

Hofstede de Groot
C. Hofstede de Groot. *A Catalogue Raisonné of the Works of the Most Eminent Dutch Painters of the Seventeenth Century. Based on the Work of John Smith*. 10 vols. London, 1907–28.

Hollstein
F. W. H. Hollstein. *Dutch and Flemish Etchings, Engravings, and Woodcuts*. Vols. 1–. Amsterdam, 1949–.

Houbraken 1718–21
Arnold Houbraken. *De Groote schouburgh der Nederlantsche konstschilders en schilderessen*. 3 vols. Amsterdam 1718–21.

de Jongh 1967
Eddy de Jongh. *Zinne- en minnebeelden in de schilderkunst van de zeventiende eeuw*. Amsterdam, 1967.

de Jongh 1971
———. "Realisme et schijnrealisme in de Hollandse schilderkunst van de zeventiende eeuw." In Brussels, Musées Royaux d'Art et d'Histoire, *Rembrandt en zijn tijd*, 1971, pp. 143–94.

Kettering 1997
Alison McNeil Kettering. "Ter Borch's Ladies in Satin." In *Looking at Seventeenth-Century Dutch Art: Realism Reconsidered*, edited by Wayne Franits, pp. 98–115. Cambridge, 1997. Originally published in Art History 16 (1993), pp. 95–124.

Kettering 2000
———. "Gerard ter Borch's Military Men: Masculinity Transformed." *In The Public and Private in Dutch Culture of the Golden Age*, ed. Arthur K. Wheelock Jr. and Adele Seeff, pp. 100–119. Newark, 2000.

Kirshenbaum 1977
Baruch D. Kirschenbaum. *The Religious and Historical Paintings of Jan Steen*. New York, 1977.

Kuretsky 1979.
Susan Donahue Kuretsky. *The Paintings of Jacob Ochtervelt (1634–1682)*, with *Catalogue Raisonné*. Oxford, 1979.

van Mander 1604
Karel van Mander. *Het Schilder-Boeck*. Haarlem, 1604.

Moiso-Diekamp 1987
Cornelia Moiso-Diekamp. *Das Pendant in der holländischen Malerei des 17. Jahrhunderts*. Frankfurt, 1987.

Montias 1987
John Michael Montias. "Vermeer's Clients and Patrons." *Art Bulletin* 69 (1987), pp. 68–76.

Montias 1989
———. *Vermeer and His Milieu: A Web of Social History*. Princeton, 1989.

Naumann 1981
Otto Naumann. *Frans van Mieris, the Elder (1635–1681)*. 2 vols. Groningen, 1981.

Playter 1972
Caroline Bigler Playter. "Willem Duyster and Pieter Codde: The 'Duystere Werelt' of Dutch Genre Painting, c. 1625–1635." Ph.D. diss., Harvard University, 1972.

Plietzsch 1936
Eduard Plietzsch. "Gabriel Metsu." *Pantheon* 17 (January–June 1936), pp. 1–13.

Plietzsch 1960
———. *Holländische und flämische Maler des 17. Jahrhunderts*. Leipzig, 1960.

Potterton et al. 1988
H. Potterton et al. *The National Gallery of Ireland: Acquisitions, 1986–88*. Dublin, 1988.

Robinson 1974
Franklin W. Robinson. *Gabriel Metsu (1629–1667): A Study of His Place in Dutch Genre Painting of the Golden Age*. New York, 1974.

Robinson 1985
———. *Gabriel Metsu: "The Letter."* Timken Art Gallery. San Diego, 1985.

Schotel 1903
G. D. J. Schotel. *Het Oud-Hollandsch huisgezin der zeventiende eeuw*. Arnhem, 1903.

Smith
John Smith. *A Catalogue Raisonné of the Works of the Most Eminent Dutch, Flemish, and French Painters*. 9 vols. and a *Supplement*. London, 1829–44.

Sutton 1980
Peter C. Sutton. *Pieter de Hooch: Complete Edition*. Oxford, 1980.

Sutton 1990
———. *Northern European Paintings in the Philadelphia Museum of Art from the Sixteenth through the Nineteenth Century*. Philadephia, 1990.

Sutton n.d.
———. *Gerard ter Borch (Zwolle 1617–1681 Deventer): Woman Sealing a Letter*. Otto Naumann, Ltd. New York, n.d.

Thoré-Bürger 1866
T. E. J. Thoré [W. Bürger]. "Van der Meer de Delft." Parts 1–3. *Gazette des Beaux-Arts*, 1st ser., 21 (1866), pp. 279–330, 458–70, 542–75.

Valentiner 1930
W. R. Valentiner. *Pieter de Hooch*. Klassiker der Kunst in Gesamtausgaben, vol. 35. Stuttgart, 1930.

Waagen 1854
G. F. Waagen. *Treasures of Art in Great Britain*. 4 vols. London, 1854.

Westermann 1997
Mariët Westermann. *The Amusements of Jan Steen: Comic Painting in the Seventeenth Century*. Zwolle, 1997.

Wheelock 1981
Arthur K. Wheelock Jr. *Jan Vermeer*. New York, 1981.

Wheelock 1995
———. *Vermeer and the Art of Painting*. New Haven and London, 1995.

Wieseman 2002
Marjorie Elizabeth Wieseman. *Caspar Netscher*. Doornspijk, 2002.

Ydema 1991
Onno Ydema. *Carpets and Their Datings in Netherlandish Paintings, 1540–1700*. Zutphen, 1991.

Exhibitions

Amsterdam 1976
Amsterdam, Rijksmuseum. *Tot Leering en Vermaak: betekenissen van Hollandse genrevoorstellingen uit de zeventiende eeuw*. 1976.

Amsterdam/Boston/Philadelphia 1987–88
Amsterdam, Rijksmuseum, *Masters of Seventeenth-Century Dutch Landscape Painting*, also shown at the Museum of Fine Arts, Boston, and the Philadelphia Museum of Art, 1987–88.

Amsterdam 1989–90
Amsterdam, Rijksmuseum. *De Hollandse fijnschilders: van Gerard Dou tot Adriaen van der Werff*. 1989–90.

Amsterdam 2000
Amsterdam, Rijksmuseum. *The Glory of the Golden Age. Dutch Art of the 17th Century: Paintings, Sculpture and Decorative Art*. 2000.

Dulwich/Hartford 1998–99
Dulwich Picture Gallery. *Pieter de Hooch 1629–1684*. Also shown at Hartford, Connecticut, Wadsworth Atheneum. 1998–99.

Frankfurt 1993
Frankfurt, Schirn Kunsthalle. *Leselust. Niederländische Malerei von Rembrandt bis Vermeer*. 1993.

Haarlem/Worcester 1993
Haarlem, Frans Halsmuseum. *Judith Leyster: Schilderes in een mannenwereld*. Also shown at Worcester, Massachusetts, Worcester Art Museum. 1993.

The Hague/Münster 1974
The Hague, Mauritshuis. *Gerard ter Borch, Zwolle 1617–Deventer 1681*. Also shown at Münster, Landesmuseum. 1974.

The Hague/San Francisco 1990–91
The Hague, Mauritshuis. *Great Dutch Paintings from America*. Also shown at the Fine Arts Museums of San Francisco. 1990–91.

Leiden 1966
Leiden, Stedelijk Museum de Lakenhal. *Gabriel Metsu*. 1966.

Leiden 1988
Leiden, Stedelijk Museum de Lakenhal. *Leidse Fijnschilders*. 1988.

Madrid 2003
Madrid, Museo Nacional del Prado. *Vermeer y el Interior Holandés*. 2003.

New York/London 2001
New York, The Metropolitan Museum of Art. *Vermeer and the Delft School*. Also shown at London, National Gallery. 2001.

Osaka 2000
Osaka Municipal Museum. *The Public and the Private in the Age of Vermeer*. 2000.

Philadelphia/Berlin/London 1984
Philadelphia Museum of Art. *Masters of Seventeenth-Century Dutch Genre Painting*. Also shown at Berlin, Gemäldegalerie, and London, Royal Academy of Arts. 1984.

Washington/The Hague 1995–96
Washington, National Gallery of Art. *Johannes Vermeer*. Also shown at The Hague, Mauritshuis. 1995–96.

Washington/Amsterdam 1996–97
Washington, National Gallery of Art. *Jan Steen: Painter and Storyteller*. Also shown at Amsterdam, Rijksmuseum.

Photography Credits

Cat. 36, detail